To the cybersecurity warriors, IT leaders, and business executives who stand on the frontlines of digital defense—this book is for you. Your commitment to resilience and innovation keeps the world moving forward, even in the face of cyber adversity. Keep securing, keep protecting, and keep leading the way.

Table of Contents

Introduction

In today's interconnected world, where businesses rely heavily on digital operations, cybersecurity is no longer just a precaution—it is a necessity for survival. Cyber threats are evolving at an alarming rate, targeting businesses of all sizes, from small startups to multinational corporations. A single attack can lead to catastrophic consequences, including prolonged downtime, financial losses, and irreparable reputational damage.

This book is designed to guide you step by step through the critical components of cyber resilience. Unlike traditional cybersecurity, which focuses solely on preventing attacks, cyber resilience takes a broader approach—it prepares businesses not only to defend against cyber threats but also to recover quickly with minimal disruption when an attack occurs.

Through this comprehensive guide, you will learn practical strategies to protect your organization, mitigate risks, and ensure business continuity even in the face of relentless cyber threats. Each chapter builds upon the last, providing clear, actionable steps that anyone—whether a business owner, IT professional, or security enthusiast—can implement.

By the time you finish this book, you will have a complete understanding of how to anticipate cyber risks, strengthen your defenses, and establish a well-structured recovery plan. The goal is not just to keep hackers out but to ensure that even when breaches occur, they do not cripple your operations. Let's embark on this journey to achieving t

PART 1: THE FOUNDATION OF CYBER RESILIENCE

Chapter 1: Understanding Cyber Resilience

In today's digital age, businesses rely heavily on technology to operate efficiently, serve customers, and store critical data. However, as technology advances, so do cyber threats. Hackers, cybercriminals, and even human errors pose significant risks to organizations, potentially causing system failures, data breaches, and operational disruptions.

This is where **cyber resilience** comes into play. Cyber resilience is an organization's ability to prepare for, withstand, respond to, and recover from cyber threats, ensuring minimal impact on business operations.

Unlike traditional cybersecurity, which focuses mainly on preventing attacks, cyber resilience acknowledges that breaches and disruptions are inevitable. Instead of just fortifying defenses, it ensures businesses can **continue operating even when under attack or experiencing a cyber incident**.

A **cyber-resilient organization** is one that:

- Anticipates and prepares for potential cyber threats.
- Can sustain critical functions even during a security breach.
- Recovers quickly and learns from incidents to improve future security.

Key Components of Cyber Resilience

Cyber resilience is built on a **proactive and strategic approach** to handling cyber risks. It typically includes the following elements:

- **Risk Identification and Assessment** – Understanding vulnerabilities, threat sources, and the potential impact of cyber incidents.
- **Robust Cybersecurity Measures** – Implementing security tools, policies, and best practices to reduce the likelihood of attacks.
- **Incident Response Planning** – Preparing structured steps for handling cyber incidents to minimize damage.
- **Business Continuity and Disaster Recovery** – Ensuring that critical business functions can continue despite cyber disruptions.
- **Continuous Improvement and Adaptation** – Learning from attacks and updating security strategies accordingly.

Cyber resilience is **not just a technology issue**; it involves people, processes, and policies working together to ensure that cyber threats do not cripple a business.

Cybersecurity vs. Cyber Resilience – What's the Difference?

Cybersecurity and cyber resilience are closely related, but they have distinct differences in their approach and goals.

Cybersecurity: The Focus on Protection

Cybersecurity is the practice of **protecting systems, networks, and data** from cyber threats. It involves using technologies like **firewalls, antivirus software, intrusion detection systems (IDS), and encryption** to create strong defenses against hackers, malware, and other cyber risks.

7

However, cybersecurity has **limitations** because no defense system is perfect. Even the best security measures can be bypassed by:

- **Sophisticated cyberattacks** (e.g., zero-day vulnerabilities or advanced persistent threats).
- **Insider threats**, where employees or contractors intentionally or accidentally expose data.
- **Human errors**, such as weak passwords or phishing scams.

Cyber Resilience: The Focus on Continuity

Cyber resilience takes cybersecurity a step further. It assumes that **cyber incidents will happen at some point**, and organizations must be **prepared to respond, recover, and keep operating**.

While cybersecurity focuses on **preventing** attacks, cyber resilience ensures that an organization can **withstand and recover from** attacks when they occur.

Key Differences Between Cybersecurity and Cyber Resilience

Feature	Cybersecurity	Cyber Resilience
Primary Goal	Preventing cyber threats	Ensuring business continuity after attacks
Approach	Defense-based (firewalls, antivirus, encryption)	Recovery-based (incident response, backup, business continuity)
Assumption	Threats can be blocked entirely	Some attacks will succeed, so preparation is necessary
Focus Areas	Protecting networks, data, and devices	Maintaining operations, quick recovery, and risk adaptation
Scope	Mostly technical (IT security tools, policies)	Holistic (includes people, processes, and security strategies)

Cyber resilience does not replace cybersecurity; instead, **it complements and enhances it**, ensuring that businesses do not crumble in the face of cyber incidents.

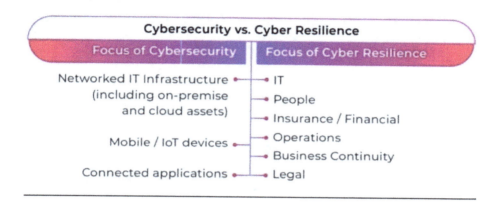

Cybersecurity vs. Cyber Resilience	
Focus of Cybersecurity	Focus of Cyber Resilience
Networked IT Infrastructure (including on-premise and cloud assets)	IT
	People
	Insurance / Financial
Mobile / IoT devices	Operations
	Business Continuity
Connected applications	Legal

Why Every Business Needs Cyber Resilience

Regardless of size, industry, or location, **every business is a potential target for cyber threats**. Cybercriminals are constantly developing new attack techniques, and no organization is completely immune.

Without **strong cyber resilience**, a single security breach can lead to:

- **Financial Losses** – Cyberattacks can cost businesses millions in ransom payments, data recovery, and legal fees.
- **Operational Disruptions** – Downtime caused by an attack can halt business activities, leading to lost productivity and revenue.

- **Reputational Damage** – Customers lose trust in companies that experience data breaches, which can result in lost business.
- **Legal Consequences** – Many businesses must comply with cybersecurity regulations like **GDPR, CCPA, or ISO 27001**, and failing to do so can result in heavy fines.

The Consequences of Cyber Attacks on Growth Industries

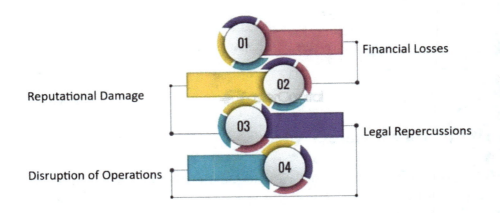

Real-World Examples of Businesses Affected by Cyberattacks

- **The Equifax Data Breach (2017)** – A cyberattack exposed the personal data of **147 million people**, leading to **lawsuits and billions in damages**.

- **The Colonial Pipeline Ransomware Attack (2021)** – A ransomware attack forced the largest U.S. fuel pipeline to shut down, causing a fuel shortage and economic disruption.

Small Businesses & Ransomware – Many **small businesses** have gone bankrupt due to ransomware attacks because they lacked cyber resilience strategies.

By implementing cyber resilience measures, businesses can **reduce the impact of cyberattacks** and recover quickly, ensuring continued operations and customer trust.

Real-World Example: A Business That Survived a Major Cyberattack

To understand the importance of cyber resilience, let's look at a real-world example of a company that successfully **recovered from a major cyberattack**.

The Attack: Ransomware Strikes a Healthcare Provider

A mid-sized healthcare provider was hit by **a ransomware attack**, encrypting all patient records and disabling its IT systems. The attackers demanded a **large ransom payment** to restore access.

The Response: A Cyber Resilience Plan in Action

Fortunately, the company had **a well-planned cyber resilience strategy**, which allowed it to recover quickly:

- **Incident Detection & Response** – The IT security team detected the ransomware infection early and **activated the incident response plan**.
- **System Isolation** – Infected systems were immediately disconnected from the network to **prevent further spread** of malware.
- **Data Recovery** – The company had **regular backups stored offline**, allowing it to restore patient records without paying the ransom.
- **Business Continuity Plan** – While IT systems were being restored, **manual processes were temporarily implemented**, allowing medical services to continue.
- **Lessons Learned & Improvements** – After recovering, the company strengthened its **cybersecurity training, endpoint protection, and backup procedures**.

The Outcome: Minimal Downtime and No Ransom Payment

Because of its **cyber resilience plan**, the company was able to **resume operations within 48 hours**, avoiding financial loss and reputational damage.

This example highlights the power of cyber resilience: **preparation and response can make the difference between business survival and catastrophic failure**.

Final Thoughts

Cyber resilience is no longer an **optional** strategy—it's a **necessity** for businesses in today's digital landscape. By understanding **what cyber resilience is, how it differs from cybersecurity, and why it is crucial**, organizations can take proactive steps to protect themselves from the inevitable cyber threats they will face.

Chapter 2: The Growing Cyber Threat Landscape

The Rise of Cyber Threats in the Digital Age

The digital revolution has transformed the way businesses operate, communicate, and store information. From cloud computing to remote work environments, organizations now rely on digital infrastructure more than ever. While this evolution brings numerous advantages, it also exposes businesses to an expanding range of cyber threats.

In today's interconnected world, cyberattacks have become more frequent, sophisticated, and damaging. Cybercriminals no longer target only large corporations; small businesses, government agencies, and even individuals face constant threats. As technology advances, so do the techniques used by hackers, making it essential for businesses to understand the evolving cyber threat landscape.

Cyber threats can disrupt business operations, cause financial loss, compromise sensitive data, and erode customer trust. Without a robust cybersecurity strategy, companies risk suffering irreversible damage. In this chapter, we will explore the most common types of cyber threats that cause downtime and discuss their potential impact.

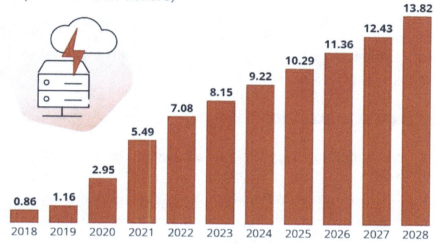

Cybercrime Expected To Skyrocket

Estimated annual cost of cybercrime worldwide (in trillion U.S. dollars)

Year	Value
2018	0.86
2019	1.16
2020	2.95
2021	5.49
2022	7.08
2023	8.15
2024	9.22
2025	10.29
2026	11.36
2027	12.43
2028	13.82

As of Sep. 2023. Data shown is using current exchange rates.
Source: Statista Market Insights

Types of Cyber Attacks That Cause Downtime

Cyberattacks come in various forms, each designed to exploit vulnerabilities in an organization's digital defenses. Some attacks are automated and widespread, while others are carefully crafted to target specific businesses. The following are the most common types of cyber threats that can lead to business disruptions and operational downtime:

- Ransomware, Malware, and DDoS Attacks

Ransomware Attacks

Ransomware is one of the most destructive forms of cyberattacks. It is a type of malware that encrypts a victim's data, rendering it inaccessible until a ransom is paid to the attacker. Hackers often demand payments in cryptocurrency, making transactions difficult to trace. Businesses that fail to have proper backups or security measures in place may face significant operational downtime or even permanent data loss.

How Ransomware Attacks Happen:

- A user unknowingly clicks on a malicious email attachment or link.
- The ransomware infiltrates the system and encrypts files.
- A ransom demand appears on the screen, instructing the victim on how to make payment.
- If the ransom is paid, the attacker may (or may not) provide a decryption key.

The best defense against ransomware includes frequent data backups, employee training, and proactive cybersecurity measures.

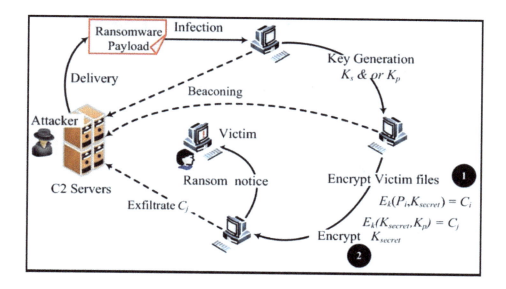

Malware Attacks

Malware (short for "malicious software") includes viruses, worms, Trojans, and spyware that infiltrate systems to steal data, disrupt operations, or grant unauthorized access. Some malware variants operate silently in the background, collecting sensitive information without detection.

Common Signs of Malware Infection:

- Slow system performance
- Unusual pop-up messages
- Unauthorized access to sensitive files
- Sudden crashes or restarts

Businesses should implement endpoint security solutions and regularly update their software to prevent malware infections.

DDoS (Distributed Denial-of-Service) Attacks

DDoS attacks aim to overwhelm a website or network with massive amounts of traffic, causing it to crash or become inaccessible. These attacks can cripple online services, leading to revenue loss and customer dissatisfaction.

How DDoS Attacks Work:

- Hackers infect multiple computers or IoT devices with malware.
- These compromised devices form a botnet, controlled remotely.
- The botnet floods a target server with excessive traffic, causing service disruptions.
- To mitigate DDoS attacks, businesses should use traffic filtering, load balancing, and anti-DDoS services.

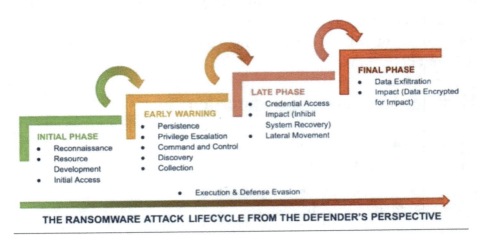

THE RANSOMWARE ATTACK LIFECYCLE FROM THE DEFENDER'S PERSPECTIVE

Phishing & Social Engineering Attacks

Phishing Attacks

Phishing is a deceptive tactic where cybercriminals trick users into revealing sensitive information, such as login credentials or financial details. Attackers often impersonate legitimate organizations through fraudulent emails, fake websites, or phone calls.

Common Phishing Techniques:

- **Email Spoofing:** Fake emails that appear to come from trusted sources.
- **Spear Phishing:** Highly targeted phishing attacks aimed at specific individuals or organizations.
- **Smishing & Vishing:** Phishing through SMS (smishing) or voice calls (vishing).

To protect against phishing, employees should be trained to recognize suspicious emails, verify sender identities, and avoid clicking on unknown links.

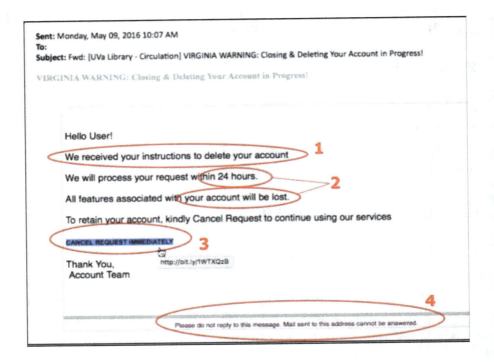

Social Engineering Attacks

Social engineering exploits human psychology rather than technical vulnerabilities. Attackers manipulate individuals into divulging confidential information or performing actions that compromise security.

Common Social Engineering Tactics:

- **Pretexting:** Creating a fake scenario to trick victims into providing information.
- **Baiting:** Luring victims with free software or gifts that contain malware.

- **Tailgating:** Gaining physical access to restricted areas by following authorized personnel.

Organizations can combat social engineering by fostering a strong security culture and implementing strict access controls.

Insider Threats and Human Error

Insider Threats

Not all cyber threats originate from external attackers. Employees, contractors, or business partners with access to sensitive data can pose significant risks, either intentionally or unintentionally.

Types of Insider Threats:

- **Malicious Insiders:** Employees who deliberately steal or leak company data.
- **Negligent Insiders:** Users who unknowingly compromise security through poor practices.
- **Compromised Insiders:** Employees whose accounts are hacked and used for malicious purposes.

To reduce insider threats, businesses should enforce least-privilege access, monitor user activity, and implement data loss prevention (DLP) solutions.

5 Types of Insider Threats

Collusive Threats

Malicious Threats

Intentional

Third-party Threats

Unintentional

Human Error

Many cyber incidents result from human mistakes, such as weak passwords, accidental data exposure, or misconfigured security settings. Employees may fall victim to phishing scams, inadvertently installing malware or sharing confidential data with unauthorized parties.

To minimize human error, companies should provide regular cybersecurity training and enforce strong security policies.

Case Study: A Company That Suffered a Cyberattack and Its Aftermath

To illustrate the real-world impact of cyber threats, let's examine a company that experienced a devastating cyberattack and how it managed the aftermath.

Case Study: XYZ Corporation's Ransomware Nightmare

XYZ Corporation, a mid-sized financial services firm, relied heavily on its IT infrastructure to process transactions and manage customer accounts. One morning, employees found themselves locked out of the company's network, with a ransom demand appearing on all screens. The attackers had encrypted critical business data, halting operations completely.

How the Attack Happened:

- A phishing email disguised as an invoice was sent to an employee.
- The employee clicked the malicious attachment, allowing ransomware to spread.
- Within hours, all company files were encrypted, and access was denied.
- The attackers demanded a hefty ransom in Bitcoin for decryption keys.

Aftermath and Recovery:

- **Business Disruption:** The company's operations came to a standstill, causing financial losses and reputational damage.
- **Response Strategy:** IT teams isolated infected systems and restored data from backups.
- **Security Overhaul:** XYZ Corporation implemented stricter email security, enhanced employee training, and adopted a zero-trust security model.

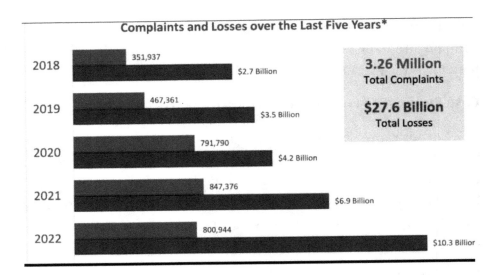

Complaints and Losses over the Last Five Years*

Year	Complaints	Losses
2018	351,937	$2.7 Billion
2019	467,361	$3.5 Billion
2020	791,790	$4.2 Billion
2021	847,376	$6.9 Billion
2022	800,944	$10.3 Billion

3.26 Million
Total Complaints

$27.6 Billion
Total Losses

This case underscores the importance of cybersecurity awareness, robust incident response planning, and proactive defenses to mitigate cyber threats.

PART 2: BUILDING A CYBER RESILIENCE FRAMEWORK

Chapter 3: The Key Pillars of Cyber Resilience

The Four Pillars of Cyber Resilience

Cyber resilience is a proactive and strategic approach to ensuring that businesses and organizations can withstand, recover from, and adapt to cyber threats and disruptions. Unlike traditional cybersecurity, which focuses mainly on preventing attacks, cyber resilience takes a broader view—accepting that some attacks will inevitably occur and ensuring that businesses can continue to operate even in the face of adversity.

To build a strong cyber resilience strategy, organizations must focus on **four key pillars**:

- **Anticipate – Identifying and Assessing Cyber Risks**
- **Withstand – Strengthening Defenses Against Attacks**
- **Recover – Responding to and Mitigating Damage**
- **Adapt – Learning from Attacks and Improving Security**

Each of these pillars plays a crucial role in ensuring business continuity and reducing the impact of cyber threats. Let's examine each pillar in detail.

1. Anticipate – Identifying and Assessing Cyber Risks

The first step in cyber resilience is **anticipation**—understanding the types of cyber risks that could threaten an organization and taking proactive measures to prepare for them. This involves identifying vulnerabilities, assessing risks, and implementing preventive measures to reduce the likelihood of an attack.

Key Aspects of Anticipation:

- **Risk Identification:** Organizations must analyze their **digital assets, networks, and data** to identify potential weak points. These could include unpatched software, outdated security protocols, or lack of employee training.
- **Threat Intelligence:** Cyber threats evolve constantly. Staying informed about **emerging threats, attack trends, and industry-specific risks** helps organizations anticipate possible breaches.
- **Regular Security Audits:** Conducting frequent security assessments and penetration testing ensures that vulnerabilities are identified before hackers can exploit them.
- **Employee Awareness Training:** Human error is one of the biggest cybersecurity risks. Training staff to recognize phishing emails, avoid suspicious links, and practice safe browsing habits strengthens an organization's ability to anticipate attacks.

2. Withstand – Strengthening Defenses Against Attacks

Once potential risks are identified, the next step is to **withstand** cyber threats by reinforcing security defenses. This ensures that even if an attack occurs, its impact is minimized.

Key Aspects of Withstanding Cyber Threats:

- **Network Security Measures:** Implementing strong **firewalls, intrusion detection systems (IDS), and endpoint protection** to block malicious activity before it reaches critical systems.
- **Multi-Factor Authentication (MFA):** Requiring multiple verification steps for accessing sensitive data significantly reduces unauthorized access risks.
- **Zero Trust Security Model:** Adopting a **Zero Trust approach** means that no one inside or outside the network is

automatically trusted—access is granted only when necessary.

- **Data Encryption:** Encrypting sensitive data ensures that even if it is stolen, attackers cannot easily read or misuse it.
- **Redundant Systems:** Having **backup systems and alternative IT infrastructure** in place ensures that businesses can continue operating even if their primary systems are compromised.

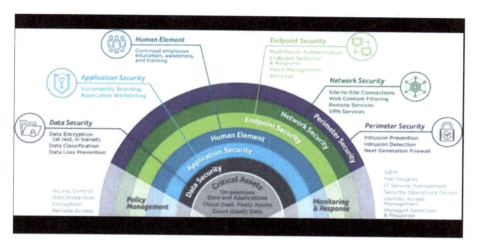

3. Recover – Responding to and Mitigating Damage

No system is 100% secure, and despite the best defenses, cyber incidents can still happen. The ability to **recover quickly** from an attack is essential for business continuity.

Key Aspects of Recovery:

- **Incident Response Plan (IRP):** A well-documented response plan outlines the **exact steps to take when a cyber incident**

occurs. This includes isolating affected systems, notifying stakeholders, and containing the breach.

- **Disaster Recovery Plan (DRP):** This plan ensures that essential systems and data can be **restored quickly** with minimal downtime.
- **Backup and Restore Procedures:** Regularly backing up important data ensures that **data loss is minimized**. Cloud-based and offsite backups are particularly valuable in case of ransomware attacks.
- **Crisis Communication Strategy:** Cyber incidents can affect **customer trust and brand reputation**. Having a transparent communication strategy to inform clients, partners, and employees is critical.

4. Adapt – Learning from Attacks and Improving Security

The final pillar of cyber resilience is **adaptation**—learning from security incidents and continuously improving cybersecurity measures. Organizations must treat each cyber event as a learning experience to strengthen future defenses.

Key Aspects of Adaptation:

- **Post-Incident Analysis:** Conducting a detailed investigation into the attack helps identify what went wrong and how it can be prevented in the future.
- **Updating Security Policies:** Cyber threats evolve rapidly. Regularly updating **security policies and procedures** ensures that an organization stays ahead of new threats.

- **Implementing Lessons Learned:** Taking corrective actions based on previous incidents **reduces the likelihood of a repeat attack**.
- **Continuous Employee Training:** Cybersecurity awareness programs should be ongoing, ensuring that employees are always informed about the latest threats and safe practices.

How to Conduct a Cyber Resilience Readiness Assessment

To determine how prepared an organization is for cyber threats, conducting a **Cyber Resilience Readiness Assessment** is essential.

This assessment helps businesses evaluate their current security posture, identify vulnerabilities, and create a plan for improvement.

Steps to Conduct a Cyber Resilience Readiness Assessment:

Identify Critical Assets:

- List **all essential systems, applications, and data** that are crucial for business operations.
- Identify which assets, if compromised, could cause the most damage.

Assess Current Security Measures:

- Review **existing cybersecurity policies, access controls, and encryption methods**.
- Conduct **penetration testing and vulnerability scans** to identify weaknesses.

Evaluate Incident Response and Recovery Plans:

- Determine if the organization has a **documented incident response plan**.
- Assess how quickly systems can be restored in the event of an attack.

Analyze Employee Readiness:

- Conduct **cybersecurity awareness training assessments** to gauge employee knowledge.
- Identify gaps in employee security practices and provide additional training.

Test Business Continuity and Disaster Recovery Plans:

- Simulate **cyberattack scenarios** to test the effectiveness of recovery plans.
- Ensure that backup and restore procedures are working correctly.

Monitor and Improve:

- Regularly review and update security measures based on **new threats and past incidents**.
- Implement continuous monitoring tools to detect potential threats in real time.

Cyber-security Self-assessment

This self-assessment assists an organization in identifying areas that need to be strengthened to help ensure security of the organization's data systems and networks. Be sure to assign action items to specific individuals or groups and follow-up to make sure that corrective actions are implemented.

Completed by: _____ Title: _____ Date: _____ Signature: _____

ITEM	YES	NO	DEPT./ VENDOR	COMMENTS	ACTION ITEMS	ASSIGNED TO
1. Has your organization, at any time during the past 12 months, experienced a cyber-incident (hacking, intrusion, malware infection, fraud loss, breach of personal information, extortion, etc.) or experienced a lawsuit or other formal dispute (with either a private party or government agency) arising from a cyber-incident?						
2. Does every device in your organization have anti-virus and anti-malware software installed and do you keep this software up to date?						
3. Do you install all relevant security patches on every system in your environment (e.g., desktops, laptops, mobile devices, servers, firewalls, routers, switches, etc.)?						
4. Do any third parties have access to your network?						
5. Do third parties use multifactor authentication when connecting to your network?						
6. Do you review the security of third parties to ensure that they have industry standard security controls in place to protect your data?						
7. Do you have firewalls in place between your network(s) and the Internet?						
8. Is your network flat (any device can talk to any other device) or segmented (devices are split by category or sensitivity to limit with which devices they can communicate?)						

Sample Self-Assessment

Final Thoughts

Cyber resilience is not a one-time effort but a continuous process. By focusing on the four pillars—**Anticipate, Withstand, Recover, and Adapt**—organizations can minimize the impact of cyber threats and ensure long-term business stability. Conducting a **Cyber Resilience Readiness Assessment** provides a clear picture of strengths and weaknesses, allowing businesses to refine their security posture over time.

By taking a proactive approach, organizations can **reduce downtime, protect sensitive data, and maintain trust with customers and stakeholders** even in the face of evolving cyber threats.

Chapter 4: Implementing a Cyber Resilience Strategy

Cyber resilience is not something that happens by accident. It requires careful planning, proactive strategies, and a structured approach to ensuring that an organization can withstand, respond to, and recover from cyber threats. In this chapter, we will explore how to build a robust cyber resilience plan step by step, align with industry-recognized frameworks such as NIST, create a risk management strategy, and prioritize critical systems and data for protection.

Developing a Cyber Resilience Plan Step-by-Step

A cyber resilience plan is a structured approach that helps organizations prepare for, respond to, and recover from cyber incidents while minimizing operational disruptions. This plan ensures that cybersecurity is not just about preventing attacks but also about sustaining business operations despite security breaches.

Step 1: Establish Cyber Resilience Objectives

Before implementing any strategies, an organization must clearly define its cyber resilience objectives. These objectives should answer key questions such as:

- What are the most critical business functions that need protection?
- What level of cyber risk is acceptable for the organization?
- How quickly should the organization be able to recover from a cyber incident?
- What are the legal and regulatory requirements the organization must comply with?

By answering these questions, an organization can establish clear goals that align with its business needs.

Step 2: Identify and Assess Cyber Risks

Once objectives are defined, the next step is to identify potential cyber threats and assess the risks they pose to the organization. This includes:

- **Identifying potential threats** (e.g., malware, phishing, insider threats, ransomware, DDoS attacks, etc.).
- **Evaluating vulnerabilities** in IT infrastructure, networks, applications, and human factors.
- **Assessing the impact** of different threats on business operations.
- **Prioritizing risks** based on likelihood and potential damage.

A thorough risk assessment helps organizations allocate resources efficiently and focus on the most critical threats.

Step 3: Develop and Implement Protective Measures

To strengthen cyber resilience, organizations must implement a set of protective measures, including:

- **Network security**: Firewalls, intrusion detection systems, and segmentation.
- **Endpoint protection**: Antivirus software, multi-factor authentication, and device management.
- **Data protection**: Encryption, access controls, and secure backups.
- **User awareness training**: Educating employees about phishing, social engineering, and password hygiene.

These measures reduce the likelihood of cyber incidents and minimize damage if an attack occurs.

Step 4: Create an Incident Response and Recovery Plan

No system is 100% secure, so organizations must have a well-defined plan to respond to cyber incidents effectively. The incident response plan should include:

- **Detection mechanisms** to identify security breaches quickly.
- **Immediate response actions** such as isolating affected systems and containing the threat.
- **Communication protocols** for notifying key stakeholders.
- **Recovery procedures** to restore affected systems and data from backups.

This step ensures that businesses can recover with minimal downtime after an attack.

Step 5: Test, Monitor, and Continuously Improve

A cyber resilience plan is not a one-time effort—it requires ongoing testing, monitoring, and updates. Organizations should:

- **Conduct regular cybersecurity drills** to test their incident response readiness.
- **Monitor security logs and alerts** to detect potential threats.
- **Review and update the cyber resilience plan** to adapt to evolving threats.

Continuous improvement is key to maintaining strong cyber resilience over time.

Aligning with the NIST Cybersecurity Framework

One of the most effective ways to implement a cyber resilience strategy is by aligning with the **NIST Cybersecurity Framework (CSF)**. This framework provides a structured approach to managing cybersecurity risks and improving resilience. It consists of five core functions:

1. Identify

This function involves understanding the organization's assets, risks, and vulnerabilities. Organizations should:

- Maintain an inventory of all IT assets, applications, and sensitive data.
- Conduct a risk assessment to identify potential threats.
- Define roles and responsibilities for cybersecurity.

2. Protect

Protection involves implementing safeguards to prevent cyber incidents. This includes:

- Enforcing access controls and multi-factor authentication.
- Encrypting sensitive data to prevent unauthorized access.
- Training employees to recognize cyber threats.

3. Detect

Detecting cyber threats quickly can prevent widespread damage. This step includes:

- Setting up continuous security monitoring tools.
- Establishing automated alerts for suspicious activities.
- Conducting regular security audits and vulnerability assessments.

4. Respond

An effective response minimizes damage and speeds up recovery. Organizations should:

- Define clear incident response procedures.
- Assign responsibilities to a dedicated response team.
- Establish communication plans for notifying affected parties.

5. Recover

The final step focuses on restoring operations after an incident. Organizations must:

- Implement backup and disaster recovery solutions.
- Evaluate and learn from incidents to improve future resilience.
- Update cybersecurity policies based on lessons learned.

By adopting the NIST framework, organizations can systematically strengthen their cyber resilience.

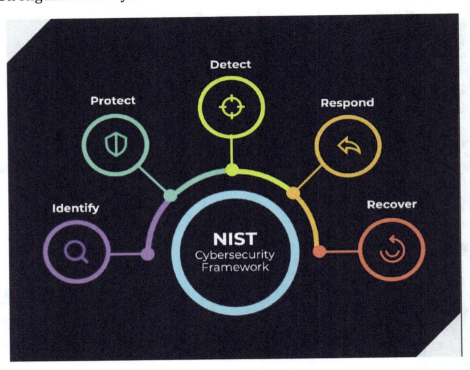

Creating a Risk Management Strategy

Cyber risk management is essential for reducing vulnerabilities and ensuring business continuity. A strong risk management strategy involves:

1. Identifying Critical Risks

Organizations must identify the risks that pose the greatest threat to their operations. This includes assessing:

- The likelihood of different cyber threats.
- The potential impact of security incidents.
- Weak points in IT systems and processes.

2. Assessing and Prioritizing Risks

Once risks are identified, they must be assessed and prioritized based on:

- **Likelihood** (How probable is the risk?)
- **Impact** (How severe would the damage be?)
- **Mitigation feasibility** (How easily can it be prevented or managed?)

3. Implementing Risk Controls

After prioritizing risks, organizations should implement measures such as:

- **Technical controls**: Firewalls, encryption, security patches.
- **Administrative controls**: Security policies, user training.

- **Physical controls**: Secure access to IT equipment and data centers.

4. Continuously Monitoring and Updating Risk Management Practices

Cyber threats evolve constantly, so risk management should be an ongoing process. Organizations should:

- Regularly reassess risks and update security measures.
- Conduct periodic cybersecurity drills and simulations.
- Stay informed about emerging cyber threats.

Likelihood \ Impact	Negligible	Minor	Moderate	Significant	Severe
Very Likely	Low Med	Medium	Med Hi	High	High
Likely	Low	Low Med	Medium	Med Hi	High
Possible	Low	Low Med	Medium	Med Hi	Med Hi
Unlikely	Low	Low Med	Low Med	Medium	Med Hi
Very Unlikely	Low	Low	Low Med	Medium	Medium

How to Prioritize Critical Systems and Data for Protection

Not all data and systems have the same level of importance. To build an effective cyber resilience strategy, organizations must identify their most critical assets and ensure they receive the highest level of protection.

Step 1: Identify Mission-Critical Systems and Data

Organizations should determine:

- Which systems and applications are essential for business operations?
- What data is most valuable or sensitive (e.g., financial data, customer records, intellectual property)?

Step 2: Classify Data Based on Sensitivity

Data should be categorized based on its importance, such as:

- **Confidential** (e.g., trade secrets, customer data)
- **Internal use only** (e.g., employee records, internal communications)
- **Public** (e.g., website content, marketing materials)

Step 3: Implement Enhanced Security for High-Priority Assets

For the most critical systems and data, organizations should:

- Use strong encryption methods.

- Implement multi-factor authentication.
- Restrict access based on roles and need-to-know principles.

Step 4: Regularly Review and Update Protection Measures

Cyber resilience requires continuous monitoring and adaptation. Organizations should periodically:

- Conduct security audits.
- Test disaster recovery procedures.
- Update security policies based on new threats.

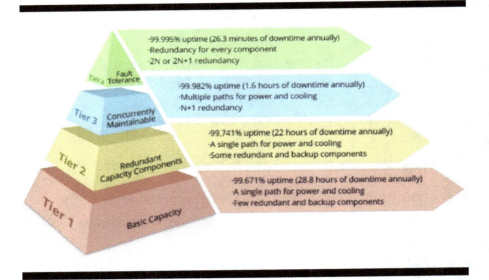

By following these steps, organizations can build a cyber resilience strategy that minimizes risk, prevents downtime, and ensures long-term security.

PART 3: PREVENTING DOWNTIME THROUGH PROACTIVE SECURITY

Chapter 5: Strengthening Security to Minimize Business Disruptions

Cyberattacks can strike at any moment, causing disruptions, financial losses, and damage to your business reputation. To ensure business continuity, organizations must proactively strengthen their security posture. This chapter explores essential best practices for preventing cyberattacks, the importance of Multi-Factor Authentication (MFA) and Zero Trust Architecture (ZTA), and how to harden your IT infrastructure. We will also walk through a step-by-step guide to setting up a secure network environment.

Best Practices for Preventing Cyberattacks

Preventing cyberattacks requires a proactive approach that includes a combination of technology, processes, and user awareness. Businesses must adopt a comprehensive security strategy to minimize vulnerabilities and ensure resilience against cyber threats.

1. Keep Software and Systems Updated

One of the simplest yet most effective security practices is keeping all software, operating systems, and applications up to date. Cybercriminals exploit vulnerabilities in outdated software to gain unauthorized access.

- Enable automatic updates for operating systems and critical applications.
- Regularly patch security flaws in all software and firmware.
- Use a vulnerability management system to detect outdated components.

2. Conduct Regular Security Training and Awareness

Employees are the first line of defense against cyber threats. Cybercriminals often target users through phishing, social engineering, and other deceptive tactics.

- Conduct periodic cybersecurity awareness training.
- Teach employees to identify suspicious emails and links.
- Implement phishing simulations to test employees' response to attacks.

3. Implement Strong Password Policies

Weak passwords are a major security risk. A strong password policy helps protect sensitive accounts from brute force and credential-stuffing attacks.

- Enforce complex password requirements (minimum of 12 characters, mix of letters, numbers, and symbols).
- Require password expiration and prevent reuse of old passwords.
- Encourage the use of password managers for storing credentials securely.

4. Limit User Access Based on Roles

The principle of least privilege (PoLP) ensures that users and systems only have access to the resources necessary for their tasks.

- Grant access only to what is needed for a user's role.
- Use role-based access control (RBAC) to define permission levels.
- Regularly review and update user permissions to prevent unnecessary access.

5. Enable Network Monitoring and Threat Detection

Continuous monitoring helps detect and respond to potential security threats before they escalate.

- Deploy security information and event management (SIEM) tools.
- Utilize intrusion detection and prevention systems (IDPS).
- Set up automated alerts for suspicious activity or unauthorized access.

Implementing Multi-Factor Authentication (MFA) & Zero Trust Architecture (ZTA)

Multi-Factor Authentication (MFA)

MFA adds an extra layer of security beyond just a username and password. By requiring additional verification, MFA significantly reduces the risk of unauthorized access, even if login credentials are compromised.

Steps to Implement MFA:

Choose an MFA Method: Options include SMS codes, authenticator apps, hardware tokens, or biometrics.

- **Enable MFA on All Critical Accounts:** Apply MFA to email, financial systems, cloud platforms, and VPNs.
- **Educate Employees on MFA Importance:** Train users to recognize and use MFA effectively.
- **Monitor and Enforce MFA Compliance:** Ensure that all users consistently use MFA for authentication.

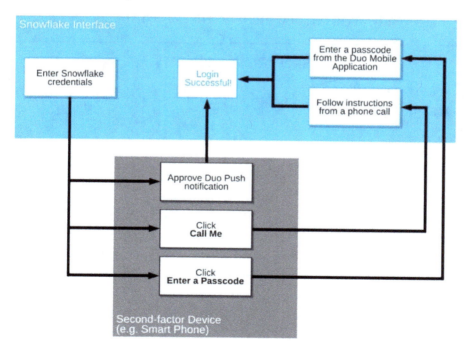

Zero Trust Architecture (ZTA)

Zero Trust is a security model that assumes no entity should be trusted by default, whether inside or outside the organization. It requires continuous verification of every request before granting access.

Key Principles of Zero Trust:

- **Verify Explicitly:** Authenticate every user and device before granting access.
- **Use Least Privilege Access:** Limit access permissions based on necessity.
- **Assume Breach:** Design the system assuming an attack has already occurred and build defenses accordingly.

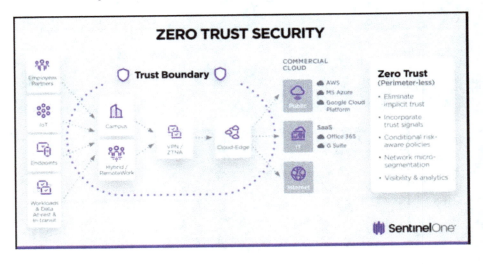

Steps to Implement Zero Trust:

- **Identify Critical Assets:** Map out sensitive data, applications, and systems.
- **Segment the Network:** Divide the IT environment into separate secure zones.
- **Require Strict Identity Verification:** Implement MFA and continuous authentication.
- **Monitor and Respond:** Use AI-powered security tools to detect threats in real time.

Hardening Your IT Infrastructure Against Threats

Hardening IT infrastructure means strengthening security at every level to reduce the risk of cyberattacks.

1. Secure Endpoints

Endpoints (computers, mobile devices, and servers) are common targets for attackers. Strengthen security by:

- Installing endpoint protection software (antivirus, anti-malware, EDR).
- Enforcing device encryption to protect stored data.
- Applying security patches and updates regularly.

2. Protect Network Perimeters

Securing the network perimeter prevents external threats from infiltrating your organization.

- Use next-generation firewalls (NGFWs) with deep packet inspection.
- Deploy intrusion prevention systems (IPS) to detect and block threats.
- Implement web filtering to prevent access to malicious websites.

3. Enforce Secure Remote Access

With remote work becoming common, secure remote access is essential.

- Require VPN connections with MFA for remote access.
- Enforce endpoint security compliance before allowing remote connections.
- Use Virtual Desktop Infrastructure (VDI) to isolate work environments.

4. Regularly Perform Security Audits and Penetration Testing

Frequent security assessments help uncover vulnerabilities before attackers exploit them.

- Conduct vulnerability scans to identify weak points.
- Perform penetration testing to simulate real-world attacks.
- Address and remediate all findings from security audits.

Step-by-Step Guide: Setting Up a Secure Network Environment

A secure network environment minimizes the risk of unauthorized access, data breaches, and operational disruptions. Follow these steps to establish a robust security framework:

Step 1: Define Network Security Policies

- Establish security policies governing user access, data protection, and system configurations.
- Ensure compliance with industry regulations and best practices.

Step 2: Implement Network Segmentation

- Divide the network into separate segments (e.g., internal, guest, production, and development networks).
- Restrict traffic flow between segments using firewalls and access control lists (ACLs).

Step 3: Deploy Firewalls and Intrusion Prevention Systems

- Configure firewalls to block unauthorized traffic and enforce security rules.
- Deploy an intrusion prevention system (IPS) to detect and mitigate threats in real time.

Step 4: Secure Wireless Networks

- Use WPA3 encryption for Wi-Fi security.
- Hide SSIDs and implement MAC address filtering for additional protection.

Step 5: Monitor and Log Network Traffic

- Deploy SIEM solutions to analyze and correlate security logs.
- Set up real-time alerts for suspicious activities and network anomalies.

Step 6: Perform Regular Security Audits

- Conduct periodic network security reviews to assess vulnerabilities.
- Update security policies and infrastructure based on audit findings.

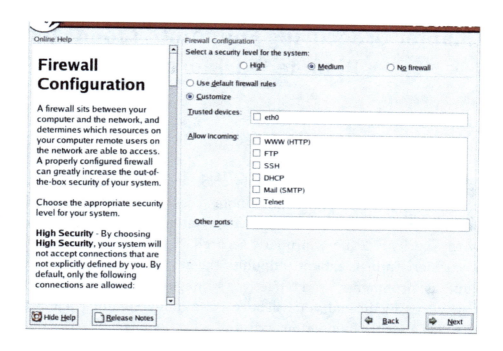

Conclusion

Strengthening security to minimize business disruptions requires a multi-layered approach that includes best practices, advanced authentication methods, IT hardening techniques, and a well-structured network environment. By implementing the strategies outlined in this chapter, organizations can significantly reduce their risk exposure and ensure operational continuity in the face of cyber threats.

Chapter 6: Securing Endpoints, Cloud, and Remote Workforces

I n today's interconnected digital world, businesses rely on various devices, cloud services, and remote access solutions to maintain productivity. However, these very systems present significant cybersecurity risks if not properly secured. This chapter will explore how cybercriminals exploit endpoints, the best practices for securing cloud environments, and effective strategies to protect remote workforces. By the end, you will have a clear understanding of how to establish a secure foundation across all access points.

How Cybercriminals Exploit Endpoints and Devices

Endpoints refer to any device that connects to a business network, such as computers, smartphones, tablets, IoT devices, and even printers. These devices are prime targets for cybercriminals because they often serve as the weakest link in an organization's security framework. Understanding how attackers exploit endpoints can help businesses implement stronger defenses.

Common Endpoint Security Threats

Malware Infections

- Attackers distribute malware through phishing emails, malicious downloads, and infected USB drives.
- Malware can steal sensitive data, disrupt operations, or provide hackers with remote access to devices.

Ransomware Attacks

- Malicious software encrypts files and demands payment for decryption.
- Ransomware often spreads through phishing, malicious email attachments, or vulnerable remote desktop services.

Phishing and Social Engineering

- Attackers trick users into revealing login credentials or installing harmful software.
- These scams often impersonate trusted contacts or organizations.

Zero-Day Exploits

- Cybercriminals take advantage of newly discovered software vulnerabilities before developers can issue patches.
- These exploits can be used to install malware or gain unauthorized access to systems.

Unsecured IoT Devices

- Smart devices with weak security settings can be hijacked and used in large-scale cyberattacks.
- Default credentials and lack of software updates make IoT devices vulnerable.

How to Strengthen Endpoint Security

- **Enable Endpoint Detection and Response (EDR):** EDR solutions continuously monitor for suspicious activity and automatically mitigate threats.
- **Implement Strong Access Controls:** Enforce least privilege access policies so that users only have the permissions they need.
- **Regularly Update Software and Firmware:** Keep operating systems, applications, and device firmware updated to patch vulnerabilities.
- **Deploy Antivirus and Anti-Malware Solutions:** Use advanced security tools that offer real-time protection against known and emerging threats.
- **Educate Employees on Cyber Hygiene:** Train staff to recognize phishing attempts and avoid unsafe browsing habits.

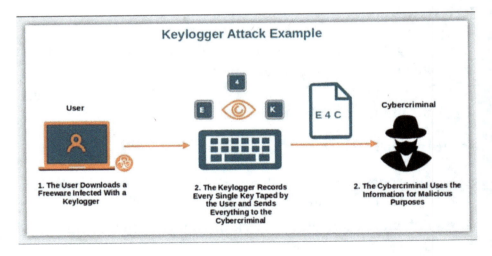

Cloud Security Measures to Protect Business Data

Cloud computing has revolutionized how businesses store, process, and access data. While cloud services offer flexibility and scalability, they also introduce security risks. Securing cloud environments requires a combination of best practices, technical safeguards, and user awareness.

<u>Key Cloud Security Threats</u>

Unauthorized Access

- Weak passwords and poorly configured authentication mechanisms can allow unauthorized users to access cloud resources.

Data Breaches

- Sensitive data stored in the cloud may be exposed due to misconfigured permissions or malicious insiders.

Misconfigurations and Human Error

- Inadequate security settings, such as open storage buckets, can lead to accidental data exposure.

Insider Threats

- Employees or third-party vendors with access to cloud systems may intentionally or unintentionally cause security incidents.

Denial-of-Service (DoS) Attacks

- Attackers can overload cloud resources, causing service disruptions and downtime.

Best Practices for Securing Cloud Environments

- **Enable Multi-Factor Authentication (MFA):** Require users to verify their identity using multiple authentication factors.
- **Encrypt Data at Rest and in Transit:** Protect sensitive information from unauthorized access by using strong encryption methods.
- **Implement Role-Based Access Control (RBAC):** Restrict access based on user roles to minimize the risk of data leaks.
- **Regularly Audit Cloud Configurations:** Continuously review security settings to detect and fix misconfigurations.
- **Monitor Cloud Activity in Real-Time:** Use security information and event management (SIEM) tools to detect suspicious activity.
- **Establish Data Backup and Recovery Plans:** Ensure that critical data is backed up and can be restored in case of a security incident.

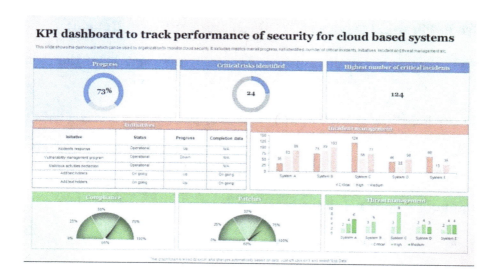

Protecting Remote Workers and Hybrid Work Environments

The shift to remote and hybrid work has expanded the attack surface for cybercriminals. Employees accessing business networks from personal devices, unsecured Wi-Fi networks, and external locations introduce additional risks. Implementing strong security measures ensures that remote workers remain productive while keeping business data safe.

Security Challenges in Remote Work

Unsecured Home Networks

- Employees working from home often use personal Wi-Fi networks that lack strong security configurations.

61

Use of Personal Devices (BYOD – Bring Your Own Device)

- Personal laptops and smartphones may not have the same security protections as company-issued devices.

Increased Phishing Attacks

- Remote employees are more vulnerable to phishing scams due to the lack of in-person verification.

Weak Endpoint Protection

- Devices without enterprise-level security software are at higher risk of malware infections.

Insecure File Sharing and Collaboration Tools

- Using unapproved file-sharing platforms can expose sensitive business data.

How to Secure Remote Workforces

- **Require VPN Usage for Secure Connections:** Employees should use virtual private networks (VPNs) to encrypt their internet traffic.
- **Provide Company-Managed Devices:** If possible, issue secure, company-controlled devices with pre-configured security settings.
- **Enforce Endpoint Security Policies:** Require employees to install security software and enable automatic updates on personal devices used for work.

- **Use Secure Collaboration Tools:** Ensure that all video conferencing, messaging, and file-sharing platforms have end-to-end encryption.
- **Implement Zero Trust Security:** Regularly verify the identity and security status of users and devices before granting access.

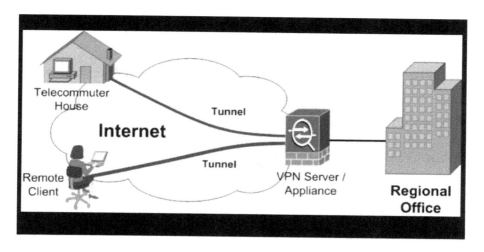

Checklist: Ensuring Security Across All Access Points

To summarize, here's a checklist to help businesses secure their endpoints, cloud infrastructure, and remote workforce effectively.

Endpoint Security Checklist

✓ Install antivirus and anti-malware software on all devices

✓ Keep operating systems and applications updated

✓ Implement multi-factor authentication (MFA) for user accounts

✓ Enforce strong password policies and regular password changes

✓ Use endpoint detection and response (EDR) solutions
✓ Encrypt sensitive data stored on endpoint devices

Cloud Security Checklist

✓ Enable encryption for data at rest and in transit
✓ Configure access control policies based on the principle of least privilege
✓ Regularly audit and update cloud security settings
✓ Monitor cloud activity and set up alerts for suspicious behavior
✓ Ensure data backups are regularly updated and securely stored
✓ Establish clear cloud security policies for employees

Remote Workforce Security Checklist

✓ Require VPN usage for remote employees
✓ Restrict access to sensitive data based on user roles
✓ Train employees on identifying phishing scams and cybersecurity threats
✓ Secure video conferencing and collaboration tools
✓ Implement device management policies for company-issued and personal devices
✓ Adopt a Zero Trust security framework for continuous verification

By implementing these measures, businesses can significantly reduce security risks and create a robust cybersecurity posture that protects their digital assets, no matter where employees or data reside.

Chapter 7: Data Protection and Backup Strategies

The Importance of Data Redundancy & Regular Backups

Understanding Data Redundancy and Why It Matters

In today's digital world, data is one of the most valuable assets for any business or individual. Losing data due to cyberattacks, hardware failures, accidental deletions, or natural disasters can be devastating. This is where **data redundancy** plays a crucial role.

Data redundancy means having multiple copies of the same data stored in different locations or formats to ensure it remains accessible even if the original version is lost or corrupted. This practice ensures that businesses and individuals can **recover lost information quickly and minimize downtime**. The more redundant your data is, the lower your risk of losing critical information.

The Role of Regular Backups

While redundancy provides protection by storing duplicate copies of data, **backups** take it a step further by maintaining **historical versions of data** over time. Regular backups ensure that even if data is lost, corrupted, or compromised due to ransomware attacks, human error, or hardware malfunctions, a clean and recent copy can be restored.

Benefits of Regular Backups:

- **Data Recovery** – Ensures lost or deleted files can be restored.
- **Protection Against Cyber Threats** – Guards against ransomware, malware, and hacking attempts.
- **Business Continuity** – Prevents costly downtime in case of system failures.
- **Compliance Requirements** – Many industries require regular backups for legal and security compliance.
- **Peace of Mind** – Knowing that data is safe allows businesses and individuals to focus on their work without fear of losing valuable information.

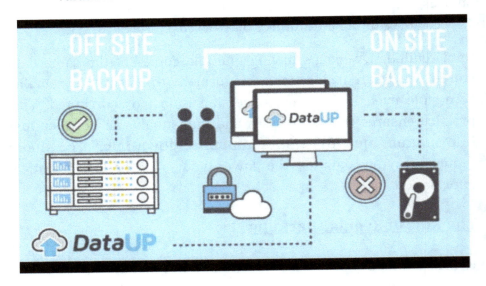

Best Practices for Data Encryption and Storage Security

Why Encryption Matters for Data Security

Data encryption is the process of converting readable data into an unreadable format that can only be accessed with a decryption key. Encryption adds an extra layer of protection, ensuring that even if unauthorized individuals gain access to your data, they cannot read or use it.

Encryption is essential for businesses and individuals because it:

- **Protects sensitive data** from cybercriminals.
- **Ensures compliance** with data security regulations.
- **Safeguards data** stored on local devices, cloud storage, and backup systems.

Best Practices for Data Encryption:

- **Use Strong Encryption Algorithms** – AES-256 (Advanced Encryption Standard) is the industry standard for securing sensitive data.
- **Encrypt Data at Rest and in Transit** – Ensure that both stored data and data being transmitted over networks are encrypted.
- **Implement Full-Disk Encryption** – Protect entire hard drives or storage devices to prevent unauthorized access.
- **Secure Encryption Keys** – Store encryption keys separately from encrypted data to prevent attackers from accessing both.

- **Regularly Update Encryption Methods** – Cyber threats evolve, so it's important to use up-to-date encryption techniques.

Secure Storage Practices:

- **Use Cloud Storage with Encryption** – Many cloud services offer built-in encryption to protect files.
- **Employ Multi-Factor Authentication (MFA)** – Adding an extra layer of security ensures that even if login credentials are stolen, attackers cannot easily access stored data.
- **Limit Access Control** – Only authorized personnel should have access to sensitive data and backup files.
- **Monitor and Audit Storage Systems** – Regularly check for security vulnerabilities and unauthorized access attempts.

Implementing a Business Continuity & Disaster Recovery Plan

What is a Business Continuity Plan (BCP)?

A **Business Continuity Plan (BCP)** is a strategy that ensures a company can continue operating in the event of a cyberattack, natural disaster, hardware failure, or other disruptions. It focuses on maintaining essential business functions, even under unexpected circumstances.

What is a Disaster Recovery Plan (DRP)?

A **Disaster Recovery Plan (DRP)** is a subset of BCP and focuses on restoring IT infrastructure, systems, and data after a major disruption. While BCP ensures business operations continue, DRP ensures that lost data and systems are recovered as quickly as possible.

Steps to Implement a Business Continuity & Disaster Recovery Plan:

- **Identify Critical Business Functions** – Determine which systems, applications, and data are essential for daily operations.
- **Assess Risks and Vulnerabilities** – Identify potential threats such as cyberattacks, power outages, or data breaches.
- **Establish Data Backup and Redundancy Procedures** – Ensure backups are frequent and stored in multiple locations.
- **Develop a Clear Recovery Plan** – Outline step-by-step procedures for restoring data and systems after a failure.
- **Test and Update the Plan Regularly** – Conduct regular simulations to ensure that recovery processes work effectively.
- **Assign a Disaster Recovery Team** – Designate personnel responsible for executing the plan during an emergency.

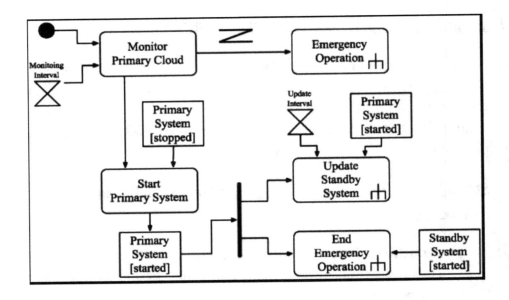

Step-by-Step Guide: How to Set Up an Effective Backup System

Setting up an effective backup system requires careful planning and execution. Below is a structured guide to ensure your data remains protected.

Step 1: Choose the Right Backup Strategy

There are several types of backups:

- **Full Backup** – Creates a complete copy of all data (best for initial backup and critical files).
- **Incremental Backup** – Backs up only new or changed files since the last backup (saves storage space and time).

- **Differential Backup** – Backs up new or changed files since the last full backup (balances speed and storage usage).

A **3-2-1 Backup Rule** is highly recommended:

- Keep **3 copies** of your data.
- Store them on **2 different storage types** (e.g., local and cloud storage).
- Keep **1 copy offsite** (for disaster recovery).

Step 2: Select a Secure Backup Location

Options include:

- **External Hard Drives** – Useful for personal and small business backups.
- **Network-Attached Storage (NAS)** – Ideal for organizations needing centralized backup.
- **Cloud Backup Services** – Provides offsite storage with encryption and automatic syncing.

Step 3: Automate the Backup Process

Manually backing up data is prone to human error. Use **backup software** to schedule automatic backups. Many tools allow daily, weekly, or continuous backups, ensuring no data is missed.

Step 4: Encrypt and Protect Backups

Since backups contain sensitive data, **encryption is essential**. Use **AES-256 encryption** and store encryption keys separately. Also, **password-protect and limit access** to backup storage.

Step 5: Test Your Backup System Regularly

A backup is only useful if it can be restored successfully. Conduct regular **backup and restoration tests** to verify:

- Files are backed up correctly.
- Data integrity is maintained.
- Recovery time meets business needs.

Step 6: Maintain Backup Logs and Documentation

Keep records of backup schedules, storage locations, and restoration steps. This documentation is crucial in the event of a cyberattack or hardware failure.

Final Thoughts

Data protection and backup strategies are vital for **business continuity and personal security**. Implementing **data redundancy, encryption, and disaster recovery plans** ensures that critical information remains **secure, accessible, and recoverable** even in the worst-case scenarios. By following best practices and maintaining an effective backup system, businesses and individuals can **minimize risks, prevent data loss, and maintain operations smoothly**.

Taking action today will save time, money, and stress in the future!

PART 4: RESPONDING TO AND RECOVERING FROM CYBER ATTACKS

Chapter 8: Incident Response – What to Do When an Attack Happens

The Cyber Incident Response Lifecycle

Cyber incidents can strike at any time, disrupting business operations, compromising sensitive data, and causing financial and reputational damage. The key to minimizing the impact of an attack is having a well-structured **Incident Response Plan (IRP)** that ensures a swift and organized response.

Incident response is not a single action but a continuous cycle of preparation, detection, containment, eradication, recovery, and learning. This structured approach is known as the **Cyber Incident Response Lifecycle**, and it consists of six critical stages:

1. Preparation

A strong incident response begins long before an attack occurs. Organizations must be prepared with clear policies, trained personnel, and the right tools. This includes:

- Developing and documenting an **Incident Response Plan (IRP)**
- Training employees on cybersecurity awareness
- Setting up **intrusion detection systems (IDS)** and **security information and event management (SIEM)** solutions

- Regularly testing response plans with **tabletop exercises** and simulations

2. Identification

Detecting a cyber threat as early as possible is crucial. Identification involves monitoring systems for unusual activities and determining if a security incident is occurring. This includes:

- Analyzing alerts from **security tools** (firewalls, IDS, antivirus software)
- Investigating reports from **employees** who notice suspicious activity
- Identifying **indicators of compromise (IOCs)**, such as unauthorized login attempts or unusual network traffic

3. Containment

Once an attack is identified, immediate action is required to prevent it from spreading and causing further damage. The containment phase is divided into two steps:

- **Short-term containment:** Quickly isolating affected systems, such as disconnecting infected devices from the network
- **Long-term containment:** Implementing patches, strengthening security controls, and ensuring the attack does not reoccur

4. Eradication

After containment, the next step is eliminating the threat from the system. This includes:

- Identifying and removing **malicious software** or compromised accounts
- Patching **vulnerabilities** that were exploited
- Conducting a thorough security audit to ensure no backdoors remain

5. Recovery

Recovery focuses on restoring normal business operations while ensuring that the attacker cannot regain access. Key steps include:

- Restoring systems from **clean backups**
- Monitoring for **any signs of persistent threats**
- Gradually bringing systems back online in a controlled manner

6. Lessons Learned

Every incident provides valuable insights that can strengthen future security measures. This phase involves:

- Conducting a **post-incident review** to analyze what went wrong
- Updating the **Incident Response Plan** based on findings
- Enhancing security policies to prevent similar attacks

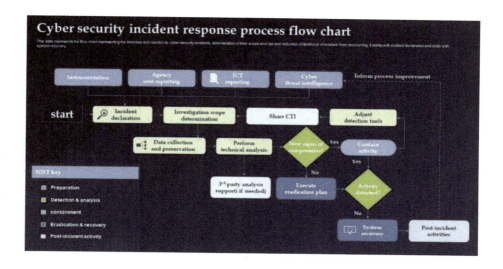

Cyber security incident response process flow chart

Step-by-Step Guide: How to Contain and Neutralize a Cyber Threat

When a cyberattack is detected, immediate action is required. The following step-by-step guide outlines how to **contain, neutralize, and recover from an attack** effectively:

Step 1: Isolate Affected Systems

- **Disconnect compromised devices** from the network to prevent the spread of malware.
- **Restrict user access** to critical systems until the threat is contained.
- **Check firewall rules** and adjust them to block malicious traffic.

Step 2: Identify the Attack Type

- Examine logs from **SIEM tools** to determine whether the attack is a **ransomware infection, phishing attempt, or insider threat**.
- Look for **unusual access patterns, data transfers, or unauthorized logins**.
- Cross-check indicators with **threat intelligence databases**.

Step 3: Secure Backup Data

- Ensure **backup files are intact and not infected**.
- If backups are stored online, **disconnect them** from the network to prevent ransomware encryption.
- Verify the latest backups before restoring.

Step 4: Eradicate the Threat

- Remove **malicious software** using advanced endpoint protection tools.
- Reset **compromised credentials** and enforce multi-factor authentication.
- Conduct a **full forensic analysis** to detect remaining threats.

Step 5: Restore and Monitor Systems

- Restore data from a **clean, pre-attack backup**.
- Gradually reconnect systems **while monitoring for suspicious activity**.
- Implement **new security measures** to prevent future attacks.

Ensuring Minimal Downtime and Quick Recovery

Cyberattacks can be disruptive, but **rapid recovery** strategies help businesses resume operations with minimal downtime. Here's how:

1. Maintain a Business Continuity Plan (BCP)

A **BCP** outlines how critical business functions will continue in the event of a cyberattack. It includes:

- **Failover systems** that switch to backup infrastructure
- Cloud-based solutions for **remote access**
- Designated **response teams** for emergency situations

2. Leverage Cloud and Redundant Systems

- Utilize **cloud-based disaster recovery solutions** that offer automated failover.
- Implement **redundant servers** to switch operations seamlessly.
- Use **virtual desktop infrastructure (VDI)** to allow employees to continue working.

3. Regularly Test Recovery Procedures

- Conduct **simulation drills** to ensure employees know how to respond.
- Test **data restoration processes** to confirm backups are effective.
- Analyze previous incidents to improve **recovery speed**.

Real-World Example: How a Business Successfully Handled a Cyber Attack

The Attack

A **medium-sized financial firm** suffered a **ransomware attack** that encrypted critical customer data. The attackers demanded **$500,000** for decryption keys.

The Response

Immediate Containment

- The firm's IT team **disconnected affected servers** from the network.
- Affected employees were instructed to **log out and stop using company systems**.

Identifying the Root Cause

- Security logs revealed that a **phishing email** had been used to deploy ransomware.
- The attacker exploited a **weak employee password** to gain access.

Eradication and Recovery

- The IT team used **forensic analysis** to remove all traces of malware.
- Backups were **verified and restored**, ensuring minimal data loss.
- Affected employees were **retrained on phishing awareness**.

Lessons Learned

- The company **implemented stricter access controls** and enforced **multi-factor authentication**.
- Regular **employee training and phishing simulations** were introduced.
- The incident response plan was **updated and tested quarterly**.

Outcome

The firm **recovered operations within 48 hours** without paying the ransom. By implementing stronger cybersecurity measures, they **prevented future attacks** and **improved their resilience**.

<u>Final Thoughts</u>

Cyber incidents are inevitable, but a strong incident response strategy can drastically **reduce damage, minimize downtime, and ensure a quick recovery**. Organizations must focus on **proactive defense, rapid containment, and continuous learning** to stay ahead of evolving threats.

By implementing a **structured incident response plan**, training employees, and maintaining **robust recovery solutions**, businesses can effectively withstand cyberattacks and emerge stronger than before.

Chapter 9: Business Continuity Planning & Crisis Management

How to Maintain Operations During and After a Cyberattack

Introduction to Business Continuity Planning

Cyberattacks are an unfortunate reality in today's digital landscape. No organization is immune to the risks posed by cybercriminals, system failures, or human errors. The key to survival is **preparation and resilience**. Business continuity planning (BCP) ensures that an organization can continue functioning, even when faced with severe cyber disruptions. It is a strategic process that involves risk assessment, contingency planning, and rapid recovery measures.

Without a well-structured business continuity plan, a cyberattack can cause prolonged downtime, financial loss, and reputational damage. However, with the right plan in place, businesses can **mitigate damage, protect critical assets, and restore normal operations as quickly as possible**.

Key Steps to Maintain Operations During a Cyberattack

- **Activate the Incident Response Plan**
  When a cyberattack occurs, the first step is to trigger the **incident response plan**. This includes identifying the nature

of the attack, assessing its severity, and containing the breach before it spreads further.

- **Isolate Affected Systems**
  Cyberattacks often spread through networks, so it's critical to **disconnect compromised systems** from the rest of the infrastructure. This may involve shutting down servers, blocking unauthorized access, or restricting affected users from certain resources.
- **Implement Emergency Communication Protocols**
  Clear and immediate communication is essential. Businesses must inform relevant stakeholders, including employees, IT teams, and management, while avoiding panic.
- **Engage Cybersecurity Experts**
  If internal teams cannot handle the situation effectively, external cybersecurity professionals should be consulted. Their expertise can help neutralize threats more efficiently.
- **Prioritize Critical Business Functions**
  During a crisis, businesses must focus on keeping their most **essential functions operational**. This could include customer service, payment processing, or core product deliveries. Backup systems and manual processes should be used where necessary.
- **Monitor for Further Attacks**
  Cybercriminals may attempt additional breaches after their first attack. Businesses should enhance security monitoring and use **intrusion detection systems** to catch any suspicious activity.

Steps to Restore Operations After a Cyberattack

- **Assess the Damage**
  Conduct a comprehensive analysis of the **extent of the attack**, including lost data, system failures, and financial impact.

- **Restore from Backups**
  If backups exist, businesses should restore operations using the **latest clean backup** before the attack occurred. Cloud backups and offsite storage solutions can be particularly valuable in these situations.

- **Reinforce Security Measures**
  After restoring operations, businesses must **patch vulnerabilities** that allowed the attack to occur. This could include updating software, enhancing firewalls, and reinforcing multi-factor authentication.

- **Conduct a Post-Incident Review**
  Every cyberattack should serve as a learning opportunity. Organizations should analyze **what went wrong, what worked well, and how they can improve future responses**.

- **Rebuild Customer Trust**
  If customer data was compromised, transparency is crucial. Businesses should **inform affected customers, provide necessary support, and reinforce confidence in their security measures**.

Creating an Emergency Response Team

Why Every Business Needs an Emergency Response Team

A cyberattack can escalate rapidly, requiring a coordinated and swift response. An **Emergency Response Team (ERT)** is responsible for mitigating damage, restoring operations, and ensuring business continuity.

The ERT should consist of professionals from different departments, including **IT, legal, operations, communications, and management**. Each member should have clear responsibilities to avoid confusion during a crisis.

Key Roles in an Emergency Response Team

Incident Commander

- Leads the response team, makes critical decisions, and coordinates actions.

IT Security Specialists

- Detect and neutralize threats, isolate infected systems, and restore data.

Legal and Compliance Officers

- Ensure that all actions comply with industry regulations and legal requirements.

Public Relations and Communication Team

- Manage internal and external communications, ensuring accurate information is relayed to stakeholders.

Human Resources (HR) Representative

- Assists employees affected by the attack and ensures proper cybersecurity training is provided post-incident.

Steps to Build an Effective Emergency Response Team

Identify Key Personnel

- Select experienced individuals who understand cyber risks and business operations.

Define Roles and Responsibilities

- Clearly outline each member's duties and expectations.

Develop an Incident Response Plan

- Establish standard operating procedures (SOPs) for different cyberattack scenarios.

Conduct Regular Training and Drills

- Simulate cyberattacks to ensure the team is well-prepared for real-life incidents.

Maintain an Updated Contact List

- Ensure all response team members can be reached immediately during an emergency.

Case Study: A Business That Recovered in Record Time

Scenario: A Ransomware Attack on a Financial Firm

A mid-sized financial company experienced a **ransomware attack** that encrypted all customer files, making them inaccessible. Cybercriminals demanded a hefty ransom in exchange for restoring access.

Immediate Actions Taken

- **Incident Response Activation**: The emergency response team was immediately deployed.
- **Network Isolation**: IT teams disconnected compromised systems to prevent the malware from spreading.
- **Communication with Authorities**: The company reported the incident to law enforcement and cybersecurity firms.
- **Backup Restoration**: Since the company had **recent, secure backups**, they restored the encrypted files without paying the ransom.
- **Strengthening Security**: Additional firewalls, endpoint security measures, and staff training were implemented to prevent future attacks.

Recovery Time

Within **48 hours**, the company was able to resume operations without major disruptions. Because of its **well-prepared business continuity plan and robust backup strategy**, it avoided financial losses and maintained customer trust.

Final Thoughts

Business continuity planning and crisis management are not just IT concerns—they are **organizational imperatives**. Companies that invest in **preparedness, response teams, and security infrastructure** will be able to withstand cyberattacks and recover with minimal impact. A strong **business continuity plan ensures resilience**, keeping the company operational even in the face of adversity.

Organizations that proactively implement these measures will **not just survive cyber threats but emerge stronger and more secure in the long run**.

Chapter 10: Legal, Compliance, and Regulatory Considerations

Understanding Cybersecurity Laws and Regulations

In today's digital landscape, businesses and organizations are required to follow a range of cybersecurity laws and regulations to protect sensitive data, prevent unauthorized access, and ensure compliance with industry standards. These laws are designed to hold businesses accountable for data protection, safeguarding customer privacy, and responding effectively to cyber threats.

Why Are Cybersecurity Laws Important?

Cybersecurity laws exist to:

- **Protect consumer data** from breaches, theft, and misuse.
- **Ensure transparency** in how businesses handle personal and financial information.
- **Set legal consequences** for companies that fail to protect sensitive information.
- **Encourage best practices** for cybersecurity measures and incident response.
- **Strengthen trust** between businesses and their customers.

Without these regulations, organizations could handle data recklessly, leading to financial fraud, identity theft, and loss of consumer trust. Laws ensure that businesses implement strong security measures, prepare for cyberattacks, and respond quickly to minimize damage.

Key Cybersecurity Laws and Regulations

Different regions and industries follow specific cybersecurity laws. Some of the most significant global regulations include:

1. General Data Protection Regulation (GDPR) (European Union)

- Applies to any business that processes personal data of EU citizens.
- Requires companies to get explicit user consent before collecting data.
- Grants users the right to access, correct, or delete their data.
- Enforces strict penalties for non-compliance.

2. California Consumer Privacy Act (CCPA) (United States - California)

- Grants California residents control over their personal data.
- Requires businesses to disclose data collection practices.
- Gives consumers the right to opt-out of data selling.
- Imposes fines for failing to comply with privacy requests.

3. ISO 27001 (International Standard for Information Security Management)

- Provides a framework for managing information security risks.
- Focuses on policies, risk assessment, and continuous improvement.

- Helps businesses build a structured security program.

4. National Institute of Standards and Technology (NIST) Cybersecurity Framework (United States)

- Designed for businesses of all sizes to improve cybersecurity posture.
- Offers a structured approach to identifying, preventing, detecting, responding, and recovering from cyber threats.
- Encourages continuous monitoring and risk management.

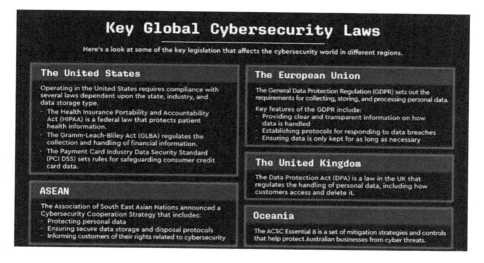

Each of these regulations has unique requirements, and businesses need to evaluate which ones apply based on their operations and the regions they serve.

Compliance Requirements for GDPR, CCPA, ISO 27001, and NIST

Compliance is more than just following rules—it's about implementing best practices that protect sensitive data and maintain operational security. Let's go over the compliance requirements for each major regulation.

1. GDPR Compliance Requirements

To comply with GDPR, businesses must:

- **Obtain explicit consent** before collecting personal data.
- **Allow users to access, modify, or delete their data** upon request.
- **Encrypt sensitive data** and implement access controls.
- **Appoint a Data Protection Officer (DPO)** if handling large amounts of data.
- **Notify authorities of data breaches** within 72 hours.
- **Conduct regular risk assessments** and implement data protection policies.

Failing to comply with GDPR can result in fines of up to **€20 million or 4% of annual revenue**, whichever is higher.

2. CCPA Compliance Requirements

Businesses that collect data from California residents must:

- **Disclose what personal data is collected and how it's used.**
- **Allow consumers to opt-out of data collection or request deletion.**

- Provide a "Do Not Sell My Personal Information" link on websites.
- Secure personal information to prevent unauthorized access.
- Train employees on privacy policies and consumer rights.

Non-compliance can lead to fines of **$2,500 per violation** or **$7,500 for intentional violations**.

3. ISO 27001 Compliance Requirements

Organizations aiming for **ISO 27001 certification** must:

- Develop an **Information Security Management System (ISMS)** that defines policies and controls.
- Perform **risk assessments** to identify potential security threats.
- Implement **access control measures** to restrict unauthorized data access.
- Conduct **internal and external audits** to ensure compliance.
- Train **employees on information security policies.**

While ISO 27001 compliance is not legally required, many businesses pursue certification to enhance their security posture and gain trust from customers.

4. NIST Cybersecurity Framework Compliance Requirements

The NIST framework is designed to improve cybersecurity across industries. Key requirements include:

- **Identifying assets and vulnerabilities** through continuous risk assessments.
- **Protecting systems with firewalls, encryption, and access controls.**
- **Detecting and responding to security incidents** using monitoring tools.
- **Recovering from cyberattacks** through data backup and business continuity plans.

NIST compliance is **voluntary**, but it provides a structured approach for businesses to strengthen their cybersecurity defenses.

The Role of Cyber Insurance in Business Protection

Even with strong cybersecurity measures in place, businesses can still fall victim to cyberattacks. This is where **cyber insurance** comes in. Cyber insurance provides financial protection by covering losses related to data breaches, business interruptions, and cyber extortion.

Why Is Cyber Insurance Important?

Cyberattacks can lead to:

- **Financial losses** from fraud, ransom payments, and legal fees.
- **Operational disruptions** that shut down business activities.
- **Reputation damage** from customer data breaches.
- **Regulatory fines** for failing to protect sensitive data.

Having cyber insurance ensures that a business can recover quickly and minimize financial damage.

Types of Cyber Insurance Coverage

First-Party Coverage – Covers direct losses to the business, including:

- Data recovery and system repair costs.
- Business interruption losses.
- Ransom payments for cyber extortion.

Third-Party Coverage – Covers damages claimed by external parties, including:

- Customer lawsuits due to a data breach.
- Regulatory fines and legal penalties.
- Liability claims for failing to secure data.

How to Choose the Right Cyber Insurance Policy

To select the best cyber insurance, businesses should:

- Assess their **level of cyber risk** based on industry and operations.
- Review what **types of attacks and losses** are covered.
- Ensure the policy includes **legal and regulatory cost coverage.**
- Consider coverage for **insider threats and employee negligence.**

Cyber insurance is not a substitute for cybersecurity measures, but it serves as a financial safety net when things go wrong.

Initial Notification
01

Post-Settlement Considerations
06

Investigation and Documentation
02

Litigation
05

Coverage Assessment
03

04
Negotiation and Settlement

Final Thoughts

Understanding and complying with cybersecurity regulations is essential for protecting both business and customer data. Regulations like **GDPR, CCPA, ISO 27001, and NIST** provide structured guidelines for securing information, while **cyber insurance** offers financial protection in the event of a cyberattack. Businesses must take a **proactive approach** by implementing strong security controls, conducting regular audits, and staying up-to-date with legal requirements. Cyber resilience is not just about technology—it's about accountability, preparedness, and trust.

Would your business be able to survive a cyberattack today? If not, now is the time to strengthen your compliance and security strategies!

PART 5: ADVANCED CYBER RESILIENCE STRATEGIES FOR THE FUTURE

Chapter 11: Threat Intelligence and AI-Driven Cyber Defense

How AI and Machine Learning Are Changing Cybersecurity

Introduction to AI in Cybersecurity

Artificial Intelligence (AI) and Machine Learning (ML) are transforming the landscape of cybersecurity, bringing new levels of automation, accuracy, and efficiency to threat detection and prevention. Traditional cybersecurity measures rely heavily on predefined rules and human intervention, which can be slow and reactive. AI-driven security systems, on the other hand, learn from vast amounts of data, recognize patterns, and predict potential threats before they cause damage.

Cybercriminals are constantly evolving their tactics, making it difficult for conventional security systems to keep up. AI and ML help bridge this gap by analyzing behaviors, identifying anomalies, and responding to cyber threats in real time. By leveraging AI, organizations can enhance their security posture, reduce response time, and minimize human errors in threat detection.

How AI and ML Work in Cybersecurity

AI-powered cybersecurity systems use algorithms and models that continuously analyze data from various sources, including network traffic, user behavior, and system logs. Here's how AI contributes to modern cybersecurity:

Threat Detection and Anomaly Identification:

- AI analyzes normal network behavior and flags any unusual activity that could indicate a cyberattack.
- ML models continuously refine their detection accuracy by learning from past incidents.

Predictive Analysis and Risk Assessment:

- AI forecasts potential threats based on historical data and emerging attack trends.
- It identifies vulnerabilities in systems before they can be exploited.

Automated Threat Response:

- AI-driven security systems can take immediate action against threats, such as isolating compromised devices, blocking malicious IP addresses, and terminating unauthorized processes.
- This reduces the need for manual intervention and speeds up response times.

Behavioral Analysis for User Authentication:

- AI enhances security measures by monitoring user behavior patterns and detecting anomalies, such as sudden changes in login locations or unusual access requests.
- This helps in preventing account takeovers and insider threats.

AI-Driven Phishing Detection:

- AI scans emails for suspicious content, links, and attachments, helping to detect phishing attempts.
- Natural Language Processing (NLP) enables AI to recognize fraudulent email patterns and alert users.

AI in cybersecurity is not a one-time implementation; it continuously evolves, adapts, and improves to keep up with new cyber threats. Organizations integrating AI into their security strategies gain a significant advantage in defending against modern cyber threats.

Using Threat Intelligence to Stay Ahead of Hackers

Understanding Threat Intelligence

Threat intelligence refers to the process of gathering, analyzing, and applying information about current and emerging cyber threats. This intelligence enables organizations to anticipate cyberattacks, strengthen defenses, and make informed security decisions.

Threat intelligence is divided into three main types:

- **Strategic Threat Intelligence:** Focuses on high-level trends in cyber threats, including motivations, attack vectors, and long-term risks.

101

- **Tactical Threat Intelligence:** Provides details on specific tactics, techniques, and procedures (TTPs) used by cybercriminals.
- **Operational Threat Intelligence:** Delivers real-time insights into ongoing cyber threats and attack campaigns.

How Threat Intelligence Helps Organizations

Using threat intelligence, organizations can proactively defend against cyber threats instead of reacting after an attack occurs. Key benefits include:

- **Early Threat Detection:** Organizations can identify and mitigate threats before they cause damage.
- **Enhanced Decision-Making:** Security teams receive actionable insights to strengthen defenses.
- **Improved Incident Response:** Faster and more effective mitigation of attacks.
- **Reduced False Positives:** AI-driven threat intelligence filters out irrelevant alerts, reducing noise for security teams.

Steps to Implement Threat Intelligence Effectively

Identify Intelligence Requirements:

- Define what information is critical for your organization's security.
- Consider threats specific to your industry and business operations.

Collect Threat Data from Multiple Sources:

- Use external sources like government agencies, cybersecurity firms, and open-source threat intelligence platforms.
- Gather internal data from security logs, network monitoring, and endpoint security tools.

Analyze and Correlate Threat Information:

- Apply AI-driven analytics to detect patterns and trends.
- Correlate findings with past attack data to predict potential threats.

Integrate Threat Intelligence into Security Systems:

- Feed intelligence into firewalls, intrusion detection systems, and Security Information and Event Management (SIEM) tools.
- Automate responses based on intelligence insights.

Continuously Update and Refine Intelligence:

- Cyber threats evolve, so security teams must regularly update intelligence sources and improve analysis techniques.

By implementing AI-powered threat intelligence, organizations can stay ahead of cybercriminals and respond to threats proactively rather than reactively.

How to Automate Cyber Defense Strategies

The Need for Automation in Cyber Defense

With cyberattacks becoming more sophisticated and frequent, manual security responses are no longer sufficient. Automated cyber defense strategies ensure faster response times, minimize human error, and enhance security efficiency.

Automation is particularly useful in areas such as threat detection, incident response, and security policy enforcement. AI-driven automation reduces the burden on security teams while improving overall protection.

Key Components of an Automated Cyber Defense System

AI-Powered Threat Detection and Response:

- AI analyzes network traffic and detects anomalies in real-time.
- Automated response actions, such as blocking malicious traffic, are executed instantly.

Security Orchestration, Automation, and Response (SOAR):

- SOAR platforms integrate various security tools, enabling automated incident response.

Example: If an employee clicks a phishing link, the system can immediately isolate their device and notify IT security.

Automated Patch Management:

- AI identifies vulnerabilities and applies security patches without manual intervention.
- This prevents exploitation of unpatched software and systems.

Self-Healing Networks and Endpoint Protection:

- AI can automatically detect and quarantine compromised endpoints.
- Self-healing systems restore affected devices by rolling back to a secure state.

Automated Compliance and Policy Enforcement:

- AI ensures that security policies are followed across the organization.
- Non-compliant devices or users can be restricted from accessing sensitive data.

Steps to Implement Automated Cyber Defense

Assess Security Needs and Identify Areas for Automation:

- Determine which security processes would benefit the most from automation.
- Focus on tasks that are repetitive, time-sensitive, or prone to human error.

Deploy AI-Powered Security Tools:

- Invest in AI-driven endpoint protection, SIEM, and SOAR solutions.

- Use automated threat intelligence platforms to enhance visibility.

Integrate Automation into Incident Response Plans:

- Define workflows for automated threat detection and response.
- Ensure that security teams can override automated actions when needed.

Continuously Monitor and Improve Automation Processes:

- Regularly assess automation effectiveness and refine response strategies.
- Ensure AI models are trained with up-to-date threat intelligence.

Train Security Teams to Work Alongside AI:

- Educate employees on how automation enhances cybersecurity.
- Train IT personnel to manage and fine-tune AI-driven security systems.

By implementing automation in cyber defense, organizations can significantly reduce response times, improve efficiency, and enhance overall security resilience.

Conclusion

AI, machine learning, and automated cyber defense strategies are revolutionizing how businesses protect themselves against modern cyber threats. By leveraging AI-driven threat intelligence and automating security responses, organizations can stay ahead of cybercriminals and ensure robust cyber resilience in an ever-evolving digital landscape.

Chapter 12: Cyber Resilience for Small vs. Large Enterprises

C yber resilience is a necessity for businesses of all sizes. Whether a small startup or a multinational corporation, every organization must safeguard its operations against cyber threats. However, the challenges, strategies, and resources available to achieve cyber resilience differ significantly between small businesses and large enterprises.

In this chapter, we will explore the unique cybersecurity challenges that small businesses face, the scalable resilience strategies that large corporations implement, and real-world examples of businesses adapting to cyber resilience effectively.

Unique Cybersecurity Challenges for Small Businesses

Small businesses are a primary target for cybercriminals due to their limited security resources and lack of advanced defenses. While they may not have as much data as large corporations, attackers know that small businesses often lack the infrastructure needed to detect, withstand, and recover from cyber incidents.

1. Limited IT and Security Budgets

Unlike large enterprises with dedicated cybersecurity teams, small businesses typically operate on tight budgets and may not allocate sufficient funds for advanced cybersecurity measures. Many small business owners believe they are too insignificant to be targeted, leading to minimal investments in security tools, employee training, and incident response planning.

2. Reliance on Basic Security Measures

Most small businesses rely on basic security measures such as antivirus software and firewalls but fail to implement comprehensive security frameworks like Zero Trust or endpoint detection and response (EDR) systems. This makes them vulnerable to phishing attacks, malware, and ransomware.

3. Lack of Cybersecurity Awareness and Training

Employees in small businesses often wear multiple hats, and cybersecurity is usually not a priority in their daily operations. A lack of formal training increases the risk of human error, which is one of the leading causes of cyber breaches. Phishing attacks, weak passwords, and improper handling of sensitive data remain common issues.

4. Increased Vulnerability to Ransomware and Phishing Attacks

Cybercriminals target small businesses with ransomware attacks because they are less likely to have robust backup and recovery strategies. A successful ransomware attack can cripple operations, resulting in data loss and financial strain. Additionally, phishing emails and fraudulent websites can trick employees into providing sensitive login credentials, leading to data breaches.

5. Difficulty in Implementing Regulatory Compliance

Small businesses often struggle with regulatory compliance due to a lack of legal and security expertise. Regulations like GDPR, HIPAA, and CCPA require strict data protection measures, but many small businesses fail to meet these standards, increasing their legal and financial risks.

How Small Businesses Can Improve Cyber Resilience

To overcome these challenges, small businesses can implement practical and cost-effective cyber resilience strategies:

- **Adopt Multi-Factor Authentication (MFA):** Enforce MFA on all business accounts to reduce unauthorized access.
- **Conduct Regular Employee Training:** Educate employees on phishing, password security, and safe online practices.
- **Implement Automated Security Tools:** Use AI-powered security solutions to detect and prevent cyber threats.
- **Regular Data Backups:** Ensure critical data is backed up frequently to mitigate ransomware risks.
- **Outsource Cybersecurity Services:** Partner with Managed Security Service Providers (MSSPs) for cost-effective security solutions.

Comparison of Cyber Risks for Small vs. Large Businesses

Cyber Risk Factor	Small Businesses	Large Businesses
Target for Cyber Attacks	More vulnerable due to limited security resources.	Targeted for high-value data and intellectual property.
Security Budget	Restricted budget, often lacks dedicated cybersecurity teams.	Larger budgets allow investment in advanced security measures.
IT Infrastructure	Simpler networks but often less protected.	Complex infrastructure with multiple layers of security.
Cybersecurity Expertise	Limited in-house expertise; often relies on third-party providers.	Access to highly skilled cybersecurity professionals and in-house teams.
Attack Methods Used	More likely to suffer from phishing, ransomware, and credential theft.	Subject to advanced persistent threats (APTs) and sophisticated hacking attempts.
Regulatory Compliance	Often unaware or struggling to meet compliance requirements.	Strictly regulated with dedicated compliance teams.
Incident Response	Slower response due to lack of resources and preparedness.	Well-defined incident response plans with dedicated SOC (Security Operations Center).
Third-Party Risk	Often depends on outsourced IT providers with varying security standards.	Uses multiple vendors but enforces stringent security policies.
Business Continuity	High risk of permanent closure after a major cyberattack.	Can recover more effectively due to backup systems and insurance.
Reputation Impact	Loss of customer trust can be devastating and lead to business failure.	May suffer reputational damage but can recover with PR and security investments.

How Large Corporations Can Scale Their Cyber Resilience Strategies

Large enterprises face a different set of cybersecurity challenges compared to small businesses. While they often have dedicated security teams, complex IT infrastructures, and higher budgets, they must also protect vast amounts of sensitive data across multiple locations and networks.

111

1. Managing a Large and Complex IT Infrastructure

Large enterprises operate across multiple offices, cloud environments, and remote locations. Ensuring consistent security policies across such a vast infrastructure is a major challenge. Cyber resilience strategies must account for diverse endpoints, network segments, and data storage systems.

2. Insider Threats and Human Risk Factors

The larger the workforce, the higher the risk of insider threats. Whether intentional or accidental, employees and third-party vendors can become security risks. Managing privileged access and ensuring employee compliance with security policies is crucial.

3. Threat Intelligence and Advanced Attack Detection

Large organizations attract more sophisticated cyber threats, including Advanced Persistent Threats (APTs) and targeted ransomware campaigns. They must invest in threat intelligence platforms, Security Information and Event Management (SIEM) systems, and real-time attack monitoring.

4. Compliance with Multiple Regulatory Standards

Multinational corporations must adhere to multiple regulations such as GDPR, CCPA, ISO 27001, and NIST frameworks. Compliance requires constant monitoring, reporting, and policy enforcement.

5. Cyber Resilience at Scale

To build cyber resilience at scale, large enterprises must implement:

- **Zero Trust Security Model:** Ensure strict identity verification and least-privilege access control.
- **Automated Incident Response:** Utilize AI-driven security orchestration tools to respond to threats in real-time.
- **Redundant Data Centers and Cloud-Based Recovery:** Maintain multiple backups across secure locations.
- **Cyber Resilience Drills:** Conduct regular attack simulations to test incident response readiness.
- **Vendor Risk Management:** Assess and mitigate cybersecurity risks associated with third-party vendors.

Case Study: How Different Businesses Adapt to Cyber Resilience

Case Study 1: Small Business Survives a Ransomware Attack

A small healthcare clinic fell victim to a ransomware attack that locked patient records and demanded a large ransom. The clinic did not have a dedicated IT team but had invested in automated cloud backups. Because of this, they were able to restore their data without paying the ransom. Key takeaways:

- **Regular cloud backups saved critical data**
- **Employee training helped identify the phishing email responsible for the attack**
- **A security consultant was brought in to improve resilience post-attack**

Case Study 2: Large Enterprise Implements AI-Driven Cyber Defense

A multinational bank with branches worldwide faced frequent phishing and DDoS attacks. To strengthen its resilience, it:

- **Implemented AI-driven threat detection systems** that blocked malicious emails in real time
- **Used behavioral analytics** to detect unusual login activity
- **Created a global security operations center (SOC)** to monitor threats 24/7

As a result, the bank saw a 60% reduction in phishing incidents and a faster response time to security threats.

Key Lessons from Both Case Studies

- **Cyber resilience is not about the size of the business but the preparedness level.**
- **Investing in backup systems and automation can save a business from complete data loss.**
- **Proactive security measures and employee training are crucial for both small and large businesses.**

Timeframe	Response Stage	Key Actions
Before an Attack (Proactive Defense)	Risk Assessment & Prevention	Conduct regular cybersecurity risk assessments, identify vulnerabilities, and implement security controls.
	Employee Training & Awareness	Educate staff on phishing scams, social engineering, and safe cybersecurity practices.
	Implementing Security Measures	Deploy firewalls, endpoint protection, multi-factor authentication (MFA), and encryption.
	Backup & Disaster Recovery Planning	Regularly back up data, test restoration procedures, and establish recovery plans.
During an Attack (Incident Response)	Threat Detection & Containment	Identify the attack, isolate affected systems, and activate the incident response team.
	Communication & Notification	Notify internal stakeholders, legal teams, and possibly affected customers or authorities.
	Mitigation & Neutralization	Remove malware, revoke compromised credentials, and apply patches or security fixes.
After an Attack (Recovery & Resilience)	System Restoration & Data Recovery	Restore systems using backups, verify data integrity, and test functionality.
	Post-Incident Analysis	Conduct a forensic investigation to understand how the breach occurred and what was compromised.
	Policy & Security Improvements	Strengthen security measures, update policies, and enhance employee training to prevent future attacks.
Ongoing (Continuous Cyber Resilience)	Continuous Monitoring & Threat Intelligence	Use security monitoring tools, conduct penetration testing, and stay updated on emerging threats.
	Regulatory Compliance & Reporting	Ensure compliance with cybersecurity regulations (e.g., GDPR, CCPA) and report incidents if required.
	Adaptive Security Strategy	Continuously evolve cybersecurity strategies based on lessons learned and threat landscape changes.

↓

Final Thoughts

While small businesses and large enterprises face different cyber resilience challenges, the core principles remain the same: **anticipate threats, withstand attacks, recover quickly, and continuously**

adapt. Small businesses should focus on cost-effective security measures, while large corporations must invest in scalable, AI-driven security frameworks. Regardless of size, businesses that prioritize cyber resilience can protect their assets, maintain operations, and safeguard their reputation in an increasingly dangerous digital world.

Chapter 13: The Future of Cyber Resilience and Emerging Threats

The Next Generation of Cyber Threats

As technology evolves, so do the threats that businesses face. Cybercriminals are continuously adapting, using more sophisticated techniques to exploit vulnerabilities. The future of cyber threats will not only involve traditional attacks like ransomware and phishing but also new and emerging dangers driven by artificial intelligence (AI), deepfake technology, quantum computing, and increasingly interconnected devices. Understanding these threats is the first step in preparing for the future.

AI-Powered Cyber Attacks

Artificial intelligence is revolutionizing industries, but it is also being weaponized by cybercriminals. AI can be used to automate attacks, making them faster, more efficient, and more difficult to detect. AI-powered malware can learn from security defenses, adapting in real time to bypass protective measures. Additionally, AI can generate highly convincing phishing emails, imitating human behavior with near-perfect accuracy. Businesses must anticipate this shift and strengthen their security frameworks accordingly.

Deepfake Technology and Social Engineering

Deepfake technology, which uses AI to create highly realistic fake videos and audio recordings, presents a major security risk. Cybercriminals can impersonate executives, employees, or trusted partners to manipulate organizations into transferring funds or sharing sensitive information. The rise of deepfake fraud means that businesses need to implement stronger verification processes and educate employees about these advanced social engineering tactics.

Quantum Computing and Cryptographic Threats

Quantum computing, while still in its early stages, has the potential to break existing encryption methods, making current cybersecurity protocols obsolete. Cybercriminals and nation-state actors could use quantum computing to crack encryption algorithms, exposing sensitive data. To stay ahead, businesses will need to transition to quantum-resistant encryption technologies, which are being developed to withstand these powerful computational threats.

The Expanding Internet of Things (IoT) Attack Surface

The growing number of connected devices increases the attack surface for cybercriminals. Smart devices, from industrial sensors to home security systems, often have weak security protections, making them easy targets for hackers. IoT-based botnets can be used to launch massive Distributed Denial-of-Service (DDoS) attacks, crippling business operations. Companies must prioritize security in IoT deployments, ensuring that devices are regularly updated and properly secured.

Supply Chain and Third-Party Risks

Modern businesses rely on a complex network of suppliers and service providers, creating multiple entry points for cybercriminals. A single compromised vendor can lead to a large-scale data breach affecting multiple organizations. Supply chain attacks, such as those targeting software providers and cloud services, will become more frequent. Businesses must enforce stringent security standards for third-party vendors and continuously monitor their supply chain for vulnerabilities.

How Businesses Can Stay Ahead in an Evolving Threat Landscape

The future of cyber resilience requires a proactive approach. Instead of merely responding to incidents, organizations must anticipate and prevent threats before they materialize. Here's how businesses can stay ahead in an increasingly hostile digital environment:

Continuous Cybersecurity Awareness and Training

The human element remains the weakest link in cybersecurity. Even the most advanced security systems can be bypassed if employees fall for phishing scams or social engineering tactics. Regular training programs should educate employees on recognizing threats, handling sensitive data, and responding to potential breaches. Simulated cyberattack drills can further enhance preparedness.

Adopting a Zero Trust Security Model

The Zero Trust approach assumes that no entity—inside or outside the network—should be trusted by default. Every access request is verified, and security measures are enforced at every level. This model minimizes the risk of insider threats and lateral movement within the network. Businesses should implement:

- Multi-factor authentication (MFA) for all users
- Network segmentation to isolate critical assets
- Continuous monitoring of user behavior for anomalies

Leveraging AI for Cyber Defense

While cybercriminals are using AI for attacks, businesses can also use AI-driven security solutions for protection. AI-powered threat detection systems analyze vast amounts of data to identify suspicious activities and respond to threats in real time. Automated security solutions can reduce response times and mitigate risks before significant damage occurs.

Enhancing Incident Response and Recovery Plans

A strong cyber resilience strategy includes a well-documented and regularly tested incident response plan. Businesses should:

- Establish a dedicated incident response team with clear roles and responsibilities.
- Conduct frequent tabletop exercises to simulate cyberattacks and test response strategies.
- Develop a communication plan for informing stakeholders, customers, and regulators in case of a breach.
- Maintain secure backups and ensure rapid restoration of critical systems.

Investing in Threat Intelligence and Collaboration

Cyber resilience is not just an internal effort—it requires collaboration. Businesses should actively engage with cybersecurity communities, threat intelligence networks, and government agencies to stay informed about emerging threats. Sharing information about attack patterns and vulnerabilities can help the entire industry improve its defenses.

Implementing Cyber Resilience Metrics

Organizations must measure their cyber resilience to continuously improve security strategies. Key metrics include:

- **Mean Time to Detect (MTTD):** How long it takes to identify a cyber threat.
- **Mean Time to Respond (MTTR):** The speed at which security teams contain and neutralize threats.
- **Recovery Time Objective (RTO):** The maximum allowable downtime before systems are restored. Regular assessments ensure that cyber resilience strategies remain effective and evolve alongside emerging threats.

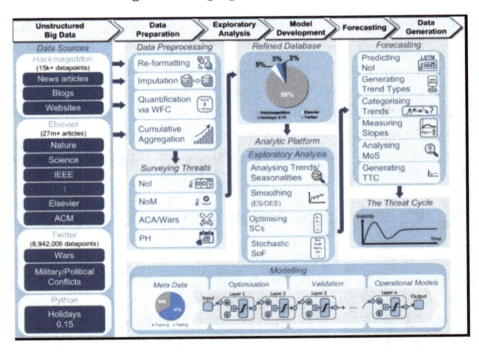

Final Recommendations for Long-Term Cyber Resilience

As cyber threats become more complex, businesses must adopt a long-term approach to cyber resilience. Here are key recommendations for ensuring sustainable security:

- **Integrate Cyber Resilience into Business Strategy**
  Cyber resilience should not be an afterthought—it must be a core part of business operations. Executives should prioritize cybersecurity investments and align them with business goals.
- **Foster a Culture of Security**
  Every employee, from entry-level staff to top executives, must understand their role in protecting the organization. Cybersecurity awareness should be embedded into the company culture.
- **Regularly Update and Patch Systems**
  Unpatched vulnerabilities are a leading cause of cyberattacks. Businesses must implement a robust patch management process to ensure all software and systems remain up to date.
- **Diversify Security Layers**
  A single security solution is not enough. Organizations should adopt a multi-layered defense approach, including firewalls, endpoint protection, encryption, and behavior analytics.
- **Plan for the Worst-Case Scenario**
  Cyber resilience is about preparing for the inevitable. Businesses should assume that breaches will occur and focus on minimizing damage and recovery time.
- **Stay Ahead of Regulatory Compliance**
  Governments worldwide are tightening cybersecurity

regulations. Businesses must stay compliant with evolving data protection laws to avoid legal consequences and financial penalties.

- **Embrace Innovation in Cybersecurity**

  As threats evolve, so must security solutions. Companies should explore cutting-edge technologies such as AI-powered defense systems, blockchain for secure transactions, and quantum-safe encryption methods.

Category	Key Takeaways	Status (✓/✗)
Risk Assessment & Planning	Conduct a comprehensive cybersecurity risk assessment.	
	Identify critical assets and potential vulnerabilities.	
	Develop and document a formal cyber resilience strategy.	
Preventive Measures	Implement multi-layered security defenses (firewalls, MFA, endpoint security).	
	Regularly update software, systems, and security patches.	
	Encrypt sensitive data to protect against unauthorized access.	
	Conduct employee cybersecurity awareness training.	
Incident Response Preparedness	Establish an incident response plan with clear roles and responsibilities.	
	Create a crisis communication plan for internal and external stakeholders.	
	Develop a rapid containment and mitigation strategy for cyber incidents.	
Business Continuity & Recovery	Maintain regular and secure data backups.	
	Test backup restoration procedures to ensure data integrity.	
	Establish a disaster recovery plan with predefined recovery time objectives (RTOs).	
Threat Monitoring & Detection	Deploy continuous network monitoring and intrusion detection systems.	
	Utilize threat intelligence to stay ahead of emerging cyber threats.	

Threat Monitoring & Detection	Deploy continuous network monitoring and intrusion detection systems.
	Utilize threat intelligence to stay ahead of emerging cyber threats.
	Conduct regular penetration testing and vulnerability assessments.
Compliance & Regulatory Alignment	Ensure adherence to cybersecurity compliance frameworks (e.g., GDPR, CCPA, ISO 27001).
	Maintain proper documentation for audits and compliance checks.
	Regularly update policies to align with evolving cybersecurity standards.
Continuous Improvement & Adaptation	Conduct post-incident reviews and update security measures accordingly.
	Foster a culture of cybersecurity resilience across all departments.
	Periodically revisit and refine cyber resilience strategies.

Checklist of **key takeaways for resilience planning**

Conclusion

The future of cyber resilience is shaped by an ever-changing digital landscape. Businesses that fail to adapt will find themselves vulnerable to increasingly sophisticated cyber threats. However, by taking a proactive approach—investing in security technologies, fostering a culture of awareness, and continuously refining resilience strategies—organizations can withstand cyber threats and ensure long-term success. Cyber resilience is not a one-time effort but an ongoing process of learning, adapting, and improving. The businesses that prioritize it today will be the ones best positioned to thrive in the digital world of tomorrow.

Appendices & Additional Resources

Glossary of Key Cyber Resilience Terms

Understanding cyber resilience requires familiarity with key terms used in cybersecurity, risk management, and business continuity. This glossary provides clear definitions for common terms to help readers build a solid foundation in cyber resilience.

A

Access Control – A security mechanism that restricts unauthorized users from accessing sensitive data or systems.

Advanced Persistent Threat (APT) – A prolonged and targeted cyberattack where an intruder gains unauthorized access to a network and remains undetected for an extended period.

Antivirus Software – A program designed to detect, prevent, and remove malicious software (malware) from computers and networks.

B

Backup – The process of creating a copy of data to restore it in case of loss, corruption, or cyberattacks.

Botnet – A network of infected computers controlled remotely by cybercriminals, often used for launching attacks like Distributed Denial-of-Service (DDoS).

C

Cyber Hygiene – Best practices that individuals and businesses follow to maintain a secure digital environment.

Cyber Resilience – The ability of an organization to prepare for, respond to, and recover from cyber threats while maintaining essential operations.

Cyber Threat Intelligence (CTI) – The collection and analysis of information about potential cyber threats to strengthen security measures.

D

Data Breach – Unauthorized access to sensitive data, often leading to data leaks or theft.

Disaster Recovery (DR) – A strategy for restoring IT systems and data after a disruptive event such as a cyberattack or natural disaster.

Distributed Denial-of-Service (DDoS) Attack – An attack where multiple compromised systems flood a targeted server or network, causing disruption.

E-G

Encryption – A method of converting data into a coded format to prevent unauthorized access.

Firewall – A network security system that monitors and controls incoming and outgoing traffic based on predefined rules.

Incident Response Plan (IRP) – A documented approach outlining steps an organization takes when responding to a cyber incident.

(Continue adding terms as needed based on the content of the book.)

Cyber Resilience Toolkit: Templates & Checklists

This section provides practical resources to help businesses implement cyber resilience strategies efficiently. The templates and checklists serve as step-by-step guides to ensure thorough preparation and response to cyber threats.

1. Cyber Resilience Readiness Checklist

A self-assessment checklist to evaluate an organization's cyber resilience preparedness.

Cyber Resilience Readiness Assessment:

✔ Do you have a documented cybersecurity policy in place?

✔ Have you conducted a risk assessment to identify potential threats?

✔ Do you have a data backup and recovery plan?

✔ Is your workforce trained on cybersecurity best practices?

✔ Have you tested your incident response plan in a real-world scenario?

2. Incident Response Plan Template

A structured template to create an effective incident response plan.

Incident Response Plan Outline:

- **Introduction** – Purpose and scope of the plan.
- **Roles and Responsibilities** – Who is responsible for responding to incidents?
- **Incident Identification** – How to recognize a cyber incident.
- **Containment Strategy** – Steps to limit the impact of an attack.
- **Eradication and Recovery** – How to remove threats and restore systems.
- **Post-Incident Review** – Lessons learned and improvements for the future.

3. Backup & Disaster Recovery Plan Template

A guide to ensure critical data and operations are protected.

Key Elements:

✓ Identify critical systems and data that need backup. ✓ Define backup frequency and storage locations. ✓ Establish roles and responsibilities for disaster recovery. ✓ Test recovery procedures regularly.

4. Security Awareness Training Checklist

A checklist to ensure employees receive proper cybersecurity training.

✓ Employees understand the importance of strong passwords.

✓ Regular phishing simulations are conducted.

✓ Secure handling of sensitive data is enforced.

✓ Remote workers follow security guidelines.

By using these resources, organizations can strengthen their cyber resilience posture and be better prepared for cyber threats. These templates can be adapted to fit specific business needs and ensure a proactive approach to cybersecurity.

www.ingramcontent.com/pod-product-compliance
Lightning Source LLC
LaVergne TN
LVHW012335060326
832902LV00012B/1898